Inner Vision

An Overcoming Story

Inner Vision

An Overcoming Story

Suzanne Gibson

Inner Vision

Who am I?

Sunny Day- Vision and Revision

I am a blind artist. This can shock some people. This is not supposed to be something that can be done. There are many blind artists, though, with varying degrees of blindness. I don't think of being an artist as an occupation one chooses. Rather it is something that chooses you. It is inside of you and needs to share itself with the world. It is more of who you are than what you do. Therefore, when you go blind, you do not stop being an artist. You only need to change the way you share yourself with the world.

Since losing my sight, I have had to trust something other than my eyes to paint. I have enough sight to see a painting, but not enough to see what I am doing as I paint. I need to 'see' the vision that I have in my mind and paint to that vision. I make changes on the canvas until what I see there is what I see in my head. Sometimes what I paint matches what I have in my head and sometimes it doesn't. I keep adjusting until the two line up.

There is something strange that happens when you lose something, some ability. There is a school of thought out there that if you lose one of your senses, others get stronger. That is not exactly true. You rely on the others more. They are exercised more and you know better how to use them. Since you are paying closer attention to them, you can better use them. This helps in compensating for what you have lost. When trying to get something done without this thing that you have lost, you need to evaluate what you have, what is now at your disposal to convey your message or accomplish your goal. You may need another tool, but you also may need to reevaluate what it is that you are trying to accomplish.

I had to learn to rely on things other than perfect sight to convey my vision. This made me evaluate what I was trying to say much more in depth than I had previously done. Before, if I wanted to paint a flower, I found one that I liked and painted it. I took the beauty that I saw and reproduced it as best as I could. Now, with sight loss, there is no way that I could simply reproduce that flower. It will not look the same no matter what I do. I need to accept that and figure out what it is that I am trying to convey. What is it about that flower that I want you to see? What is its story?

I am painting moments now, not flowers. These moments have feelings. When I paint now, I consider those feelings and how best to get you to feel them. Do the shapes need to change? What about the colors? I change both anywhere I can to get you to feel, to see, the vision that I have. I know that all great artists have inner vision and that is what they put on their canvases, but I needed to lose some of my physical vision to find all of my own inner vision.

I think all people that we call visionaries have a trust in something. Maybe it is their intellect, or luck, but most will go out on a limb not because they have a guarantee, but because they trust somehow that it will work out. I put my trust in the Spirit of God. I trust that He will guide me as I paint, write or otherwise create. I trust that He has equipped me to do the task at hand no matter the difficulty. This does not mean that I am denying reality, pretending that I do not have limitations, but that I will be able to find a way around the obstacles to accomplish my goal. I am accepting my physical limitations as obstacles, but I am not accepting that I cannot conquer them.

My husband, Chris, and I have been working on a project for our church, redoing the pre-K area. We are making 3-D art to create the feeling of being in a backyard. Eight-foot tall sculpted trees, 3-D grass, animals and more. This has been a very involved project and has required many different things to be done to accomplish our goal. There are many things along the way that I have simply not been able to do. When I paint a canvas, I use high powered magnification as well as somewhat of an impressionist style to make my vision come to life. This project is basically story-book illustration style. There are large areas of grass or trees that are painted in solid color. We are cutting out 8-foot sections of 2-layer grass that will be installed to line the hallway as well as other areas. Solid is my worst enemy. If I paint these cut-outs, Chris will need to come back and redo them since I will not see all the places where I missed. This has not turned out to be a practical way to do things, dirtying up brushes and paint trays just to have to do it again. In addition, since our creations are life-sized, I cannot fit them under my magnifier. This leaves me at a real disadvantage.

We discovered that if we worked together, I could do a first coat and hand the brush or roller to him for the second coat. I still can't get the work done on my own, but when we work together, I can significantly cut down on the time Chris needs to spend on it. I am now a valid help in the project. We also discovered that I could put the animal cut outs under the magnifier and get the base painting done. These pieces were small enough for me to work with my magnifier. This would not work for all of what we were creating, but I could do some of it. We are not doing things the way we would if I could see. I am not doing as much on my own. We are getting things done, and I am doing some of it. I am able to do something positive for my church as I am doing so for myself as I create.

Sometimes getting the vision across means getting help, sometimes it means changing the way you do things. The main point is that in order to get your vision across to others you will need to trust in some inner strength. Relying on this may make you vulnerable to failure, but those who do nothing, gain nothing. You cannot win if you do not play. Without the possibility of failure, there is no chance of success. These are all things that I say to my students to encourage them in their efforts. I say them to myself to encourage myself as well.

Contents

Parasol

Chapter One

The Early Years

Hawkeye – Vision and Revision

Stargardt's was starting to attack me when I was in my forties. I have my suspicions, though, that even when I was a child it was there affecting me. I can remember being very little and even though I knew it wasn't true, I would explain it as if I could see air. It was as if I was seeing static on an old tube TV. I saw it, mostly, when it was bright. When the sun was shining into the room brightly, I would 'see' this fuzz. This fuzz was not dust, it was made of light. It may have had nothing to do with Starguardt's, but I wonder.

At this early age, my inner vision was being fostered mostly by my parents. I was always encouraged in my artwork even as a child. I especially remember two pictures I did in kindergarten that were still on the mantel piece when I graduated high school. One was covered in yellow, orange and red spots of paint making fall leaves and then painted in black were tree trunks and branches. The other was on brown construction paper. The trees again were black, crayon this time, and on one side of every branch and tree trunk was a white line, again in crayon, depicting snow. My mother had these pictures framed and prominently placed which made me think they must have some value.

I also remember there being a painting in our family room that was painted by my great grandfather. Looking through some trees you could see a mountain in the distance. Behind our house we had an open field with a patch of trees in the middle and a lake off in the distance. I know this scene had nothing to do with the scene in the paining but somehow, I saw a correlation between the two. I felt a connection to this painting, like I could enter into it. I could imagine myself playing among the trees in this painting like I played in the trees behind my house. I know this painting spoke to me and told me from a very early age that you did not have to be some

2

celebrated, famous artist to paint. I think it told me that I could do it too.

I remember so much time spent alone drawing, coloring, cutting, gluing, anything I could do to be creative. I even used to cut the fringe off of my orange bedspread to use in my creations. (Sorry, Mom) At my grandparents' house there weren't many toys, but there was a can of crayons. I would spend hours there with those crayons and some paper making a pattern and coloring it in. It didn't matter that I had done it so many times before. I just kept making more.

I always seemed to get presents for birthdays and Christmas that revolved around creating. Paint by numbers, weaving loom kits and I even remember getting the invisible woman model which seemed a bit weird to me but it was something to build, something to make. I got a Spirograph. I spent hours making designs with it. I must have gone through tons of paper. I had a TV in my room, and I did watch it often, but I think I spent more time making things. Once I made a paper airplane out of the shiny gold foil back of an old Christmas card for my little brother. I put it in his stocking on Christmas. I painted seashells and rocks. I learned to crochet. I made things for everyone, every chance I could.

I was always well stocked with things to create with. I had many kits to make things like pot holders or hook rugs, but your basic trash would suit me as well. All the adults in my life must have recognized that there was something inside of me that needed to be expressed. I am grateful that they saw it and fostered it. My dad even added an easel top to the desk that I had in my room, making it more of an art table. As I got a little older, I was never lacking in professional art supplies. I had the big portfolio. Then I got the smaller, professional one for interviews. I had the big art box and it was stocked well. My parents didn't have gobs of money, but they placed a value on my artistic growth.

The adults in my life were always encouraging in my artistic endeavors. My creations were displayed, my self confidence was fed. As I grew older, my advice was sought out in artistic decisions around the house. What color to paint the bedroom trim, how the decorative decals for our new van should be laid out, I doubt they really needed my advice, but it built me up to have my opinion to be considered to be important. Seeing that all the adults in my life valued this interest of mine encouraged me. I think that affected who I became, who I was inside, giving me confidence to be that person.

In school I was one of the ones that would stay in at recess to decorate the bulletin board for the new holiday or season coming up. It was more fun to me to do that than to run around outside. We would cut shapes out of construction paper and make a scene appropriate for the upcoming season. I also had a lot of fun making creative projects that enhanced what we were learning about. I remember making a Native American settlement out of clay and a covered wagon out of balsa wood. I always loved it when we got to do things like that and I loved the attention that my creations got. I got a reputation at school for being one of the artistic ones and I liked that definition. So many other of the definitions that were put on me were not ones I wanted or felt good about but this one I did. The positive attention that I got for being artistic, both at home and at school, helped me define for myself who I was and who I wanted to be.

There was a time that I recall, I think it was fourth grade, that we were learning about the five senses. The teacher had us all choose one sense to lose if we had to lose one. Many chose smell, some touch or taste and a few hearing. I chose sight. Only one other boy chose the same. There was a general sense among both the teacher and other students that we chose wrong. There was not supposed to be a wrong choice. This was supposed to get us thinking about what it would be like to lose a sense, and how important they all are. Losing any sense seemed a nightmare to me, so I wasn't sure what the difference was.

At the time the show little House on the Prairie was big. Although I identified more with the tomboy Laura, I romanticized a little about the blind Mary. It intrigued me. Living this way did not seem fun and I did not want it, but I was very interested in what it would be like. I sometimes tried to walk home from school with my eyes closed. I think it was how difficult it seemed that made me so interested in it. How anyone managed their life without being able to see was fascinating. I had no idea then that I would find out for myself what it was like.

When I went to junior high school, I started to notice trouble seeing from the back of the room. I didn't really think this was trouble, I thought it was normal. It seemed to make sense to me that the farther away I was from something, the harder it was to see it. Somehow, I ended up in the back of the room very often, but I never wanted to tell the teacher that I couldn't see the board. The teachers answer to this is always to put you in the front of the room and we all know the last place a kid wants to be is in the front of the room. I would guess what was going on, I would listen to and look to others around me to help get some clues as to what was happening, but I never even admitted to the other kids that I could not see.

There was a day in science class when the teacher called on me. He had something up on the projected screen, to me it was just a giant white blur. He asked me a question and I just stood there and didn't say a word. I think he knew that I was too smart to not know the answer. I was always very good in school. I was getting by even without seeing well because I was. He asked me if I could see the screen and I told him no. He was dumbfounded as to why I wouldn't have told him and then did what I knew would happen and brought me to the front of the room.

It is probably this particular incident that drove everyone around me to figure out that I had developed nearsightedness and needed to get glasses. This really has nothing to do with Stargardt's, only with my vision. However, at the same time I can remember having difficulties recognizing people and I don't know if it was because of the nearsightedness.

I remember a time when we had taken school pictures. They handed them out in gym class but instead of just giving them to us, the teachers created a relay race. Hanging on the wall were all of our photos. We were to, on our turn, run up, grab our photo package and run back to our line. I was deathly afraid that I would not recognize myself. I never knew why that should scare me so much. Why would I not recognize myself? But now, as an adult suffering from Stargardt's, having such difficulty recognizing people I can kind of understand what might have been going on. If I could not see completely the center of my vision, recognizing people would be somewhat difficult. I was never very good at describing what people looked like. I would forget if they wore glasses, was not really sure of the color of their hair and things like that. It was usually just chalked up to my not paying attention, but now I wonder.

My teachers also recognized that I had something in me creatively that needed to be expressed. I'm sure this was partly due to the fact that all my papers had doodles and drawings lining the margins. Many of them asked me to do diagrams on their chalkboards and I always liked it when a project involved something artistic even if it was only being able to make a cover for the report that I had to do. Once I used my Dad's old style typewriter to make what we would now call a dot matrix drawing for my report cover. I can't imagine what fun I would have had with what is now available to us.

I don't exactly remember how it came to pass, I assume it must have been my ninth grade art teacher's suggestion, but in high school I applied to and got accepted in commercial art at the technical school. This class would now be called Graphic Design. With the application, we were supposed to submit several pieces of artwork. The word had gotten around that the Commercial Art teacher was a Grateful Dead fan. Along with my other submissions, I sent a skull. I think I painted it. I know it was in color. It looked more like a medical book illustration then a Grateful Dead album cover, but with no Google at the time, and not having a record to use as reference, this was the best that I could do. It is strange to think how much has changed in what seems to me, a short time. Now you would just run a search and get as many references as you could possibly want. At that time, we had to use actual items or books for reference. For those of you who don't remember, books are pieces of paper with words printed on them and then bound together. There were buildings that stored them called libraries and you could borrow these books for free.

I remember a funny side note. There was a day when anyone thinking about attending the technical school could go and visit. We were supposed to pick a first and second choice. I didn't pick a second choice. The teacher in charge came to me as we were lined up for the bus. He wanted me to pick a second choice. I told him, no way. I didn't want to go if I could not go for commercial art. He was a little taken aback by my stubbornness. He said it was only so they could schedule the day. We were all supposed to spend half the day in one class and half in another. No one was going to make me take a class that I didn't want to. I picked photography. I guess I have always been a bit strong willed, stubborn and willing to be vocal about it.

My first day I arrived at my regular school, but seeing no bus to take me to the technical school, was not sure what I was supposed to do. There was no one else waiting where the buses came and went. I went in to the homeroom teacher that I would have when attending that school to ask where I was supposed to go. He told me that he did not know and to just sit down. I sat. He went about his business and waited until homeroom was over and the other kids were on their way to their first class. He then sent me to the office. They told me that the buses for the tech school arrived later than the others and that I should have waited. Now, however, the buses were gone. I had to call my mother to come get me and take me to school.

I arrived, on my first day, to make quite an entrance. All the other students from all the other schools were there. They had already chosen their seats. The first year students were at the teacher's desk going through his orientation speech, and there I am in the classroom doorway with everyone looking at me.

I dreaded first days. I never moved, but with the structure of my overcrowded school district, changed one school or the other every year except two between sixth and twelfth grade. New kids, new teachers, new everything and I had to figure out each time where I fit in. Luckily here it did not take long for me to fit in. It was funny when after our first quarter grades came in and I got a B, a senior who was a bit full of himself told me, "Smitty doesn't give out A's." He of course got A's. I never got another B. Once I was settled into things, I took every opportunity to grow and learn everything I could. That kid never said another word to me about grades.

I attended the technical school half of each school year for my last three years of school. I would go to tech school for two weeks and then regular high school for the next two weeks and so forth. I excelled in tech school. I loved it. We not only did lessons designed to teach different techniques and concepts but as we moved in our abilities, we were allowed to do actual jobs that came to the school from businesses and organizations. I worked on posters, business cards, menu covers and even a book for burn victims. I got to go on location once and help screen print pictures on walls. I learned how to cut stencils, silk screen and to prepare for off-set printing. I learned how to select and set type on a computer and printer the size of a room. I learned proper use of a paintbrush, ink pen, exacto knife and many other things.

That room-sized computer was something. The computer was actually in a different room from the printer. It had a little window where you could see about four or five words of what you were typing on and LCD screen. Files were stored the way they are now, but we had no visual interface and that was so alien a concept to us that we often had to re-enter information because we couldn't figure out where we had saved it. Once complete, the computer would spit out a punch tape. You would then take the punch tape into the next room where the printer was. It had to be about 6-foot-tall by 3 wide and at least 8 long. You then got a disk with your font on it and opened up the printer and put it in, turn it on and pray that what comes out is what you wanted. It was printing on photo paper and the teacher that was in charge of this classroom, (not my regular class) was not happy if you wasted paper. If we got something other than what we wanted, we hid it. If he found it in the trash, you would not be allowed back to use his equipment.

The personal computer was about to burst onto the scene. We were told we were learning the industry standards, and we were. The problem was that the industry standards were about to change. Much of the technical information that we learned was obsolete just a few years after graduation. Luckily while design styles change, design concepts don't.

While there, I learned how to direct a viewer's eye to what I wanted them to see by using color and composition. The colors and placement of objects in the composition will direct your gaze to a focal point. From there you should be directed to a second and third point, traveling around the composition and ending up back at your focal point. If done well, whether in an advertisement or a piece of art, your attention will be caught, and your gaze will be fixed on the art. You will not quickly look away since you are compelled to keep following where your eye is directed. This is what makes you keep your attention focused for a prolonged period of time on a well done painting. The artist's attention to how the colors are used and where, can have you transfixed. Those colors and shapes will also affect your mood. Color plays a large role in conveying emotion, as does how calmly or chaotically objects are placed.

This experience had a lot to do with my confidence in my abilities. I dreaded having to leave after the two weeks were over and spend two weeks back in boring high school. I was made to take basic classes, some even remedial, since they had no way to put me in the advanced classes that I had been in up until that point. Twelfth grade wasn't too bad since I was able to take a photography class and was no longer required to take math, but the classes I was in for tenth and eleventh were atrocious. Coming from honors geometry, it was pretty insulting having someone try to teach me to add. It was all I could do to get through the day. I got through it by knowing that in two more weeks I would be back in my art class, working on what I loved.

My teacher in Commercial Art class was especially encouraging. He let me do as much as I was driven to do, and that was a lot. I was never happy to be working on one job at a time. I liked two or three to keep me going. When I reached a creative block on one, I would move to another. Often, I would get inspiration for a project while working on another. This allowed me to keep working with much less stress. My brain was free to keep moving, instead of stuck staring at a blank page.

One other major reason why this class changed my life so much was that is where I met my future husband. We became very good friends and eventually started dating and got married. He, being an artist too, also contributed to my artistic vision and the growth of it. I spent a lot of time hanging around Chris' desk. My seat was in front of him and he took to throwing tape balls in my hair to get my attention. I guess it worked. Since Chris was two years ahead of me, our instructor even had him show me how to do some things. He liked to have us teach each other, to help us learn by teaching. This was the beginning of our artistic relationship. We now are able to work with and consult with each other on our work so easily. We have the freedom to make comments or suggestions to each other with no offense being meant or taken. We can each, also, act on that advice or not, with no offense meant or taken. It helps us each to get the best out of each other and ourselves.

great for all of life :)

About this time my nearsightedness had gotten bad enough that it was decided I needed to wear the glasses all the time instead of just to see the board in school. This guy, this one who would become my husband, took me out to a park the day that I first wore my new, stronger glasses outside of the classroom. I was amazed to see trees on mountains, they were not just blobs, and that those trees had leaves on them. Not that I didn't know there were leaves on trees but that I could see them instead of just a green blob on a brown stick. It was amazing. Since I can no longer see these things, this is a wonderful memory. When I look at a tree now, I am back to green blobs and brown sticks. But I saw them then and since it was a new thing to me, I paid close attention. I did not take it for granted and I have them etched into my memory.

Chapter Two

Growing My Vision

Dancing Ladies – Vision and Revision

Chris and I got married a year after I graduated high school, and had three kids in the next four years. Chris was working in the silkscreen department of a sign manufacturing business, but I ended up not seeking out a job in commercial art. For the most part I spent the next season of my life being wife and mom. Because my husband too was an artist, we kept developing our artistic vision together. We had several small businesses through the years. We printed T-shirts for camps, recreational departments, lawn maintenance companies and such. To do this required creating logos, making stencils and silk-screening T-shirts. We invested in a small shirt press and a dryer. This allowed us to get a very professional product. I sourced out suppliers for the inks and T-shirts. This was not as easy as it is today. There was no internet so you could not just run a search and find what you might want. It took time, effort and luck to find the supplier that you needed. We worked out of whatever space we could. Once we printed several hundred t-shirts on my parents' back porch.

Chris, eventually took a new job as shop supervisor of a display company. One Christmas they got the job doing Macy's in store display. This year's theme was Disney's Goofy. They were to make Christmas presents in 'goofy' shapes. Since they were so overwhelmed with work wrapping these odd shaped boxes, Chris brought them home and I worked on them as well as oversaw friends and family doing them. Even the kids got involved stacking the odd shapes in packing boxes. They would actually crawl inside the giant boxes to place each one in just the right spot.

Eventually, when all the kids were in school, I took a part time job with his company in the art department. I got a lot more acquainted with famous artists works and styles as I prepared packages for potential clients.

Sometimes I would help out with the matting of art prints or with screen printing, but I did not get to exercise a whole lot of artistic expression there. I think, inside, it was still being built up. Since I had never taken any art history classes, pouring over art books was getting me familiar with different artists styles. I could now recognize a Matisse or Monet, and knew who Mondrian was. Working there also allowed me to spend a few minutes over lunch break with him. He was working such long hours that we didn't see him at home much.

I would also do things around the house to exercise my creativity. Any random day of the week, you might come in to see some piece of furniture painted or the kids' silhouettes painted on the playroom wall. If it didn't move, it might get painted. I used any paint I could get my hands on. Old wall paint was a favorite. I cut out a stencil once out of an old file folder and stenciled flowers around the ceiling of my daughter's room. Also while home, if there was someone teaching anything artistic on TV, that is what I was watching. Yes, Bob Ross, but many others as well. Oil painters, watercolorists, crafters, anything would suit me. I took all those shows, all those different techniques and parked them into my brain. I added that up with all I had learned from everywhere else and it is now there in my 'bank' to use in what I am doing. Anything you learn can be helpful to anything you do. Many things I learned watching Bob Ross were translated into techniques I used later painting murals with acrylics. His methods of making trees and nature quickly were very useful to us. You can't spend six months painting a mural. The client wouldn't be very happy, and you wouldn't be making much money. Large brushes and bold strokes went a long way for us.

I also did a lot of sewing projects at that time. One of the first things that Chris bought me was a sewing machine. I thought it was too much money to spend at the time, but he saw it as a wise investment. My grandmother's neighbor gave me a box of old scraps of fabric. Her mother had been a dress maker. She made a lot of bridesmaid dresses and her scraps were fantastic. I didn't have money for patterns, so I would lay out dresses that my daughters had, trace around them and make new dresses out of satin, velvet and lace. Some were to play dress up in, others for special occasions. Other scraps would be turned into quilts or anything else that I could figure out how to make out of what I had. Just one more way to be creative.

After about a year at the display company, Chris' old boss contacted him. The company had moved and they wanted him back. They wanted him to run the silk-screen department. We went to visit and decided to make the move. He was working such long hours at the display company and was very unhappy there. It was not an easy decision since it would take us six hours away from our family, but we thought this would be a better life for us and our kids.

After we moved I got another job, this time in a frame shop. Sometimes I would work upstairs doing the actual framing and other times I would help customers decide on colors of matting and frames to best complement their artwork. I only worked there a year, though, when things changed and my part-time position was going full-time. I could not do a full-time job, since I needed to be home after school for my kids so I left the job. It worked out since we soon decided that we would homeschool our kids. Leaving this job allowed me to do this. It ended up being a very important part of our lives.

The next ten years would be spent with my attention mainly on that. I was teacher, administrator and disciplinarian of our school. I spent each summer pouring over materials, deciding which to use to make each of my kid's year the best it could be. We joined a co-op to fill in the gaps where I needed more help. They were able to learn from others who had different strengths than mine. We also got to have a community to exist within. It meant a lot to all of us to have friends who we could share our experiences with. The kids were even able to have proms and graduation ceremonies.

I did not have any formal jobs while we were homeschooling. The family did work for a time assembling small electrical parts and later we had a paper route delivering 500 papers twice a week. These jobs allowed the kids to do all the extracurricular activities that they wanted. Skiing, ice skating, trips to museums or musicals downtown. No one liked it, but everyone was happy that the answer was always "Yes" when the question was "Can we…"

During this time, we started painting murals for people. First a neighbor asked us, knowing we were artistic, if this was something we could do. We painted a mural that wrapped around all four walls of her daughter's bedroom. We made a picket fence with flowers, animals and trees scattered around the room. After completing it we thought this might be our next business. Since I was in control of our daytime schedule, this worked out well. I could manage our school day and my work life to fit together. I was even able, as our kids got older and were capable, to take them on jobs with me and let them participate. I was able to teach them as they helped, giving both of us something that we would never have had otherwise. We had small and large projects. Anything from a small image to the entire inside of a Celtic store. This one had the walls covered in scenes of Scotland. It was our largest project. We painted a lot of kid's bedrooms. Dinosaurs, football, nature scenes and more. I even once painted a nursery for a boy that would, ten years later, come to me for art classes. Maybe his environment as a child had something to do with developing his inner vision.

I also taught a lot of art classes at our co-op, everything from elementary school through high school, enrichment through credit, charcoal drawing, pen and ink impressionism, you name it. Teaching is a wonderful way to develop things in yourself. I have always had an interest in teaching, even when I was a child. If you would ask me as a kid what I would be when I grew up, chances are I would've told you I was going to be a teacher. When other kids would ask me for an answer to a problem, rather than just giving it to them, I would try and lead them to finding it on their own. I would ask them what they thought, if this is that, then what does that mean? Showing them the way, making them think it through. Teaching.

When I wasn't teaching a class at our co-op, I was helping out in one. My kids are all very artistic and many of the classes that they took at our co-op were creative ones. Moms were always encouraged to help out in classes. Our first year, my youngest took a sewing class. She was only in third grade and I wasn't sure of her ability to use a sewing machine. She and her sister had both been doing embroidery since they were 3. They would sit and do it while waiting for their older brother while he was in preschool. Crazy, I know. It seemed normal to me at the time. Counted cross stitch was big at the time. I did a lot of it since I could do it while watching the kids play outside. I got to get some form of artistic expression out while taking care of my kids. They saw me doing it and wanted to do it too, so I taught them. It didn't seem like a big deal to me then. Since both girls had shown an ability at such an early age, I let them take the classes that interested them, including the sewing class. I assisted in this class as well as many others. I learned things, too while helping out.

I got into quilting through these sewing classes. As we all grew more capable, we started making quilts for The Quilts for Kids Foundation. This group gives quilts made by volunteers to kids in the hospital. I used to like to make 'Touchy, Feely' quilts. I had scraps of fabric of all different types. Some were meant to be for upholstery or other things than quilts. Some were rough, others silky. They all had different textures. I would cut out squares of these fabrics and sew them together into a quilt with many different textures on them. When the kids who received them were too tired to do anything else, they could just run their hands along the quilt feeling all those different textures. Each quilt we made, we thought about who might get them. Each one had a theme. Maybe cars, or birds. My daughter's and I would be inspired by the scraps that we were working with and make each one its own special design. This sounds very noble, but we were having a ball making them.

I assisted in the girl's drama classes. We would often make scenery for their plays. I also helped in the puppet class. I had a lot of fun there. We even created a puppet once for a Christmas program. It was a Christmas tree. It fit over one of the kid puppets and then shed its branches to turn into a cross. The puppet, with others sang songs through the program about Christmas and then, at the end, the puppet would shed his branches and talk about Jesus. I got a lot out of the time we had there above the connection with other home-school moms. This connection was important to me, but the ability to exercise my creativity was just as important. I actually painted several murals on the church hallway walls where we held out classes. It was always important to me to create. It didn't matter if I had no money to buy canvases and paint. There is always something to make something out of.

Chapter Three

A Downward Spiral

Highland George – See What I See

When I was in my thirties, I went to the eye doctor for a vision check up. I covered one eye, looked across the room and I saw nothing but a white blur. I was shocked and horrified. My brother had been diagnosed with Stargardt's in his early twenties. It is genetic and because he has it, there is every chance that I could have it too. I was sent off to an ophthalmologist for testing. Among other things, they injected me with a dye and took photographs of my retina. We found out that, according to them at the time, I either have it or I am carrying it. They did not know a lot about it at the time and this was not a specialist. It turns out, what they saw was that I had it. Good news at that time was that the doctor did not think this was my problem. Since by the time I got to that appointment I could see out of that eye, she said that I had had an ocular migraine. So, the scare was put off for the time being, although I knew the future might hold something different.

When our youngest turned five, she needed to get glasses for nearsightedness. Her vision went downward so quickly that she ended up in bifocals by the time she was seven. At that time, we ended up taking her to an ophthalmologist for testing too. We spent an entire day in the office with that poor little child getting every test known to man, but praise God, they decided that she did not have it. She still has terrible nearsightedness but Stargardt's has not reared its ugly head.

I was nearing forty when our kids started to graduate high school and the next season of life was upon us. We started making plans for what this next season might hold. I wanted to start painting. I had done many artistic things over the years, but never really painted anything on canvas. I painted walls, furniture and plenty of other things as well as design work, but actually painting paintings would be something new. We thought we might want to open a gallery or some kind of shop selling art. I had taken a job cleaning my church and another cooking at a daycare. Not jobs that were terribly artistic but they were helping to pay the bills, especially with two weddings coming up. Both of our girls decided to get married the same year.

As I was driving one day home from work, I was noticing that I was having trouble seeing the road signs. Figuring it was time for a new prescription I scheduled an appointment. This appointment led to another appointment at another ophthalmologist. They thought I had double vision, they thought I was colorblind. I didn't really understand how this was the answer. It didn't seem to me that my color perception had changed. I was always good at seeing color and knowing how to match it by mixing paint. I didn't think anything had changed. There were times, though, when I would have disagreements with Chris about how pink or purple something was. I took the diagnosis and deferred to others judgement on color for the time.

Before we could explore this more and figure out what was really going on, we also found out that I had a brain tumor. I had been having dizzy spells for a while and had suddenly lost about 50% of the hearing in my right ear. An MRI showed a large tumor rooted on the brain that was pressing on the balance center behind my ear. It also had snaked down to my spinal cord. This put all exploration into my visual problems on hold. Four months before the first of the two weddings I had brain surgery. On top of that, while I was still recovering this daughter that was getting married had back surgery. She was having pain from one of the rods that were put in her back when she was younger to correct Scoliosis. They needed to remove part of one. I can remember making wedding plans with the two of us in adjoining recliners, while her fiancé went back-and-forth to the computer to make changes to invitations that we, of course, were designing ourselves.

My surgery left me completely deaf in one ear and with almost debilitating tinnitus, but it did what it was supposed to do and they were able to get rid of a large portion of the tumor. The dizziness also left me immediately. They are not really sure why I can't hear. For 3 days after the surgery, I could hear. Then suddenly, nothing.

It took me ten weeks to be back to some kind of normal. I pretty much lived in my recliner. It took those 10 weeks till I was even able to lay flat to sleep in bed. My family set me up in the living room in my recliner. Extra cushions, pillows, sheets and blankets. I had a tray for meals and never left this chair except when going to the bathroom. For several days, they took me there in a wheel chair, after that they walked along side of me to make sure that I didn't fall. I was so weak it was hard to believe.

The longest walk I ever took was the one from the car to the house when they brought me home from the hospital. It was the middle of winter. My surgery had actually been on my Dad's birthday, January 28. Every year since, I tell him that for his birthday, I will not have brain surgery. We had had some snow and ice. While Chris was at the hospital getting me ready to come home, our son spent the entire morning chipping ice off our very long, steep driveway. They drove me as far as they could up the drive, right to the front walk. Our house was a bit unique, not only was there a long, steep driveway, but then you had to walk along the entire front of the house to the front door. I had to be supported by both Chris and our son to do it. I stopped half way and started to cry. I didn't think I could make it. They were afraid to carry me since it was icy and the wheelchair we had was useless since there were stairs to climb. Oh, the stairs. After making it up the front walk, which had the occasional step in it, I had to climb up four more steps. I'm not sure how, but I did it.

My mother had come to stay with us to help while I was recovering. She slept on the couch next to me so that I would never be alone. This was a good thing because I once woke up with an unbelievably terrible pain in the back of my head. She called the doctor in a panic. I told her to tell him that on a scale of 1 – 10, it was a 15. Doctors are always asking you to rate your pain on a scale of 1 - 10. Turns out, no one had told me not to lay flat. I had reclined the chair all the way and was not supposed to do that. Now that we knew, I was careful not to do that again. I spent my days and nights sitting up, ever so slightly reclined.

We had an 8t-foot-wide bow window in the living room that my recliner was facing. They set up all the flowers, cards and gift baskets in the window for me. It was amazing to see how many people reached out to me. There were many from close friends and family but also, family that I hadn't seen for ages were praying for me. Some even put me on prayer chains at their churches, so complete strangers were praying for me. All the support was very heart warming.

It is funny thinking back; I remember my mom making me fill out thank you cards. After the surgery my brain was so foggy, I couldn't see straight. I would not look at the tv since the image moved too fast and I couldn't read anything. All those cards and notes had to be read to me. But there my mom was with thank you cards. I couldn't read, let alone write, but at her insistence, I managed to at least sign my name. My handwriting must have looked atrocious. On top of not being able to see straight, I was so weak that I could barely hold the pen. I think she was just trying to put some order back into a very disorderly time.

After about ten weeks I cautiously started sleeping in bed again. I would only do it part of the night. I needed to keep testing it out to see if I was ready. Sometimes it was ok for a time, but after a bit, the pain would creep back in and I would go back to the recliner. Ever since this time, I have always cautioned people that they should make sure to have a recliner good enough to live in. You never know when it might happen to you.

I lost a lot of weight since I was not able to swallow well due to the surgery. In the hospital, I didn't really eat anything at all. Since they brought me food that I wasn't going to eat, I told my family to eat it. We didn't know it, but when they came to take the try away, they filled out a chart showing how much I had eaten. The nurses, therefore, thought that I was eating. When they found out what was going on, they brought me things like applesauce, soup and Ensure. At home, I would hear comments from one of my care takers to another like "she ate 3 pieces of peach today." This was something to be celebrated. It also was not easy since some things tasted funny. I could eat SpaghettiOs, applesauce and peaches. I'm not sure whose idea it was to try the SpaghettiOs, but these things tasted Ok to me and I was able to swallow them. I think that is pretty much what I lived on in the beginning. I could not swallow bread and baked goods tasted awful. We had some wonderful people bring over meals, and my family certainly enjoyed and appreciated it, but I don't think I ate any of them.

When my Mom went back home, I had a string of 'baby-sitters'. The first day that she was gone, I passed out on my way to the bathroom. My daughter was home, but still asleep. After that, they made sure someone was attending to me all the time. My mother came back to help with my daughters' recovery after her surgery since I was of no use to her and by the time she went home again I was able to be reliably left alone.

It was a rough road, but once I was recovered, I went back to work at the church. I don't remember when, but I had stopped working at the daycare somewhere in there along the way. I was fully back to making wedding plans, bridal shower plans and all that fun stuff. My only artistic expression at that time was pretty much these weddings, since the mural business had kind of dried up. The big box stores had started carrying wallpaper murals and for less than $100 you could get all the most popular scenes that we were doing. So table settings, shower decorations and invitations was where I put my creativity for the time.

The surgery left me with tinnitus, a small amount of trouble swallowing and deaf in one ear. The ringing in my ear was so loud and would get louder the more real noise around me was. They told me that it would go away in 3 or so months. After that they said 6 – 9. After that they said it wasn't going away. By evening each day, I couldn't take it anymore and would often be reduced to tears. I had to stay away from any noises that I could since the tinnitus would get louder to compete. I quit working at the church since running a vacuum for hours was just too noisy for me to endure.

I stopped listening to music. Music was suggested as a way to cope with tinnitus. It is called masking. Your attention is supposed to be on the music instead of the ringing. For me, the noise only got louder to compete. In the beginning, I tried to keep things as quiet as I could. Years later, I can listen to music at times, but not always and never loud. The thing that was, and still is, the hardest is the car. The road noise is a constant. When I am in the car for a long time, the tinnitus gets bad. I actually rarely notice much while in the car, but when I get out and things are quieter, there the noise is. It ramps up with outside noise, but it does not stop when that outside noise goes away. I prefer making long car trips in the evening, so I can just go to bed when we get where we are going.

After a year had gone by with no change, I was put on an anti-depressant to help me to cope. It did, but at a cost. A little bit of me died inside. It was sort of like having no feeling. Maybe things don't bother you as much, but nothing is really all that great either. After a few years I started to notice some issues. I would get into arguments with people about things. I would recount some event and everyone else would tell me that it either never happened or it didn't happen that way. I thought everyone else was nuts, I remembered. I would actually argue with my entire family over this. They were, in my opinion, collectively crazy. I remembered, and that was that. One day I looked up the side-effects of the drug that I was on and it said "an inability to accept the truth no matter what facts are presented." I stopped right there. Realizing that I was basically hallucinating, I threw the pills away and never took another one. The tinnitus is no better. I cope because I have to. I wear a noise reduction earplug in the good ear when noise is loud. Also, my brain has learned to accept it as 'normal' so my anxiety is less. Not gone, but less. If you want to know what it is like, the best description I have been able to come up with is this; imagine someone following you around holding a hairdryer to your ear. Yeah, not fun.

The swallowing is a minor annoyance. Small things are tough. Sometimes I need to turn my head to the right to get something to go down. Sometimes I need to eat something else bigger to grab what was stuck on its way down. Drinking does not help since the liquid just goes right past. Small pills can get stuck just at the top of my throat. There they will dissolve and irritate my throat if I can't get them down. I stopped taking the bread at communion in church. There were just too many times when it got stuck there and I had no way to do anything about it.

At that time, Chris was working part-time for the day care that I had worked for. He was helping them with maintenance on their properties. When their daycare burnt down, he was helping them figure out whether to rebuild or buy new. These people were very good friends of ours and knew our hearts and dreams. They found an office building much larger than they needed for their day care so, they offered us a space to use for an art gallery. Our plans for the future came a lot faster than we expected and just as the second wedding was happening, I was spending about 10 - 12 hours a day renovating this building. My strength had obviously come back full force and we were very excited. The following summer we opened our gallery and for the next six years my artistic inner vision was expressed through this gallery.

We thought a lot about what kind of place we wanted. Our motto was Art is for Everyone! We wanted a place where people could feel comfortable visiting. A place they could bring their kids and not worry about what they would see. For this reason, we decided that we would not show any nudes, tasteful or otherwise. Not from a point of condemnation of those who did, but as a way to have a space people could feel comfortable bringing their kids. I was always having to shush the giggles and calm the gasps of students when certain artworks were in books we were using or at places we were visiting. I even had to leave a place or two when I had my own kids with me and the place was just that offensive. Actually, I would have left these places on my own. It always bothered me that, somehow, the idea got out there that art is lurid. That it needs to shock people. We chose artists whose art was good quality. It may have made some kind of statement, but it was not offensive. Our gallery was one of such positivity, that I actually had a couple people ask if we were part of a church.

We also wanted to be rid of the snobbery. Many people are afraid to visit a gallery because they "don't know anything about art." We wanted a place where people did not feel judged. I always told people that all they needed to know was what they liked and that they really didn't even need to know that. They should feel free to come and look. If something moved them, it moved them. If it didn't, it didn't. I once had someone ask me what he was supposed to think about a piece. It was a photograph of an American flag. Superimposed on it was another photograph of shattered glass. The statement was about the brokenness of our country. This man wanted to know which side of the aisle this statement was. What were the politics of it? I told him that he was supposed to think whatever it made him think. A piece of art is not finished until it is viewed. You as the viewer finish the piece. The artist may have had an intent, but you bring yourself to the painting. You become part of the art and what it says to you, it says to you.

At some point along the way of all these happenings, I wrote the following to explain how I felt inside. I only wrote it for myself. Somehow, it allowed me to process and deal with my feelings. I have since shared it with others and have even done a painting to visually express it.

My Bubble

My life is a bubble, a floating bubble
>*I do not know where it will go*
>>*Will it still be here tomorrow?*
>>*Or will it be floating in some unknown place?*
>>>*It floats*
>>*It floats*

I try to tie it down,
>*but it is too slippery, I am unable to hold on to it*
>>*I stomp up and down, but I can't make it settle*
>>>*Down to the ground*
>>*It floats*
>*It floats*

The wind blows my bubble
>*I cannot control the wind*
>>*I cannot control my bubble*
>*It goes to and fro with no word from me*
>>*It floats*
>*It floats*

If you see my bubble, try to catch me
>*Try to tie my bubble down*
>>*But you can't catch my bubble*
>*My bubble floats*
>>*It floats*
>*It floats*

Chapter Four

Sight Loss

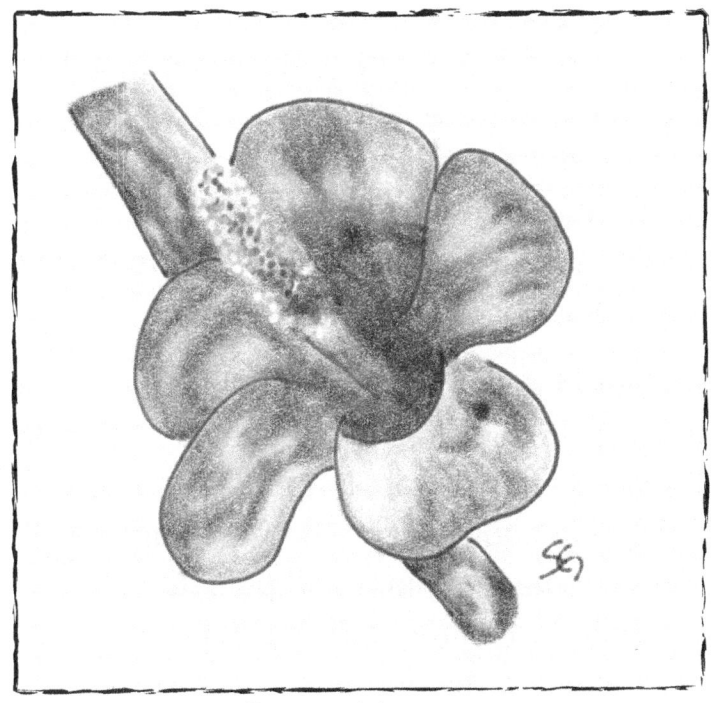

Sweet Moment

Now that I had recovered from the brain surgery, we went back to trying to figure out what was wrong with my eyes. As it turned out I was not colorblind, I did not have double vision. The Stargardt's had caught up to me. As it got worse, I could see now what was happening in my eyes. There was a ring of blur near the center of my eye. It was shaped like a Cheerio. Where the ring was, I could not see anything. So, if I was looking at a car coming down the road I would see the car, it would disappear as it hit the ring, reappear as it hit the center of the circle, disappear again as it hit the other side of the ring and then reappear again. This is why I could not read numbers in the color-blind test. I could see dots of red and green, so it was not because I couldn't see color, but because I simply couldn't see the whole image. It is also why it was appearing that I had double vision. When something was on the edge of this ring, it would appear to double.

The blur in my vision is still visible to me when I close my eyes. When closing my eyes, I see darkness except for where this blur is. It appears grayish. There is also a neon blue snowflake in the same area as the blur. It looks like it is made of light and pulsates. This could have contributed to some of the color issues. That blue would have affected my perception of pinks and purples. Not knowing that it was there, it would have mixed in with the color of what I was looking at, changing it. Now that I know it is there, I can make sure to judge color outside of the area where it affects me.

The brain is an amazing thing. In the area where I cannot see, it does not just appear black. It does not appear white or grey. I can tell you what it looks like when my eyes are closed, but when they are open, it depends on what I am looking at. If I am looking at a wall with a clock on it, I can make the clock totally disappear. The space where the clock should be looks like the wall. If the wall is dark, the space is dark, blurry but dark. If it is light, then the space is light. It is an amazing coping mechanism, but when you don't know what is going on, you miss stuff and do not know that you are missing it.

Stargardt's is an inability to process vitamin A correctly. It pools on the retina and kills the cones that you use to see. Since it is pooling in the center, you lose the center vision first. According to the Foundation for Fighting Blindness, *the retina is the delicate light-sensing tissue lining the inside wall of the back of the eye. Photoreceptor cells in the retina convert light into electrical signals, which are sent to the brain where they are processed to create the images we see. The macula, which is rich in cone photoreceptors, is responsible for sharp central vision — for tasks like reading, watching television, and looking at faces. Cones also provide vision in lighted settings and color perception.* In my case, it was actually pooling in a ring at the onset, I was able still to see in the middle of the ring. Once I knew where it was, I worked hard to keep what I wanted to see inside that ring. I could still see 20/20 there. When I didn't understand what was happening, it was hit or miss whether I could see something. Now, if I kept it in that tiny spot, I could still read small print. This would later fill in and I would be forced to compensate in other ways.

I have often been asked if there is a treatment. Many people assume that in today's world everything can be fixed by some surgery or drug. There is much research being done, but as yet no cure. No surgery would be of any help because even a new eye would just be destroyed again by the vitamin A.

You are probably wondering why we went ahead with opening a gallery when we knew that I was losing my sight. I thought, when I realized what was going on, that those days were over. I thought there was no way that I was going to be able to have the creative life that I had been waiting for. While things did not work out the way that I intended, they did work out.

One day we went to the Akron Art Museum. I noticed a few paintings that I took special note of. They appealed to me. They were portraits, but done in such an interesting way, using colors that you would not expect. It worked, though. I really liked this artist. Before we left the museum, we noticed a little room running a video. We stepped inside and found it to be about this very artist. His name was John Bramblitt and he was completely blind. When he lost his sight due to a seizure, he was so angry that he decided he wanted to paint. He did this simply because he couldn't. He had never painted before. He found a way.

On the way out of the museum, I turned to Chris and said, "I guess I don't have any excuse." John Bramblitt was completely in the black and had found a way to paint, I must be able to do the same, since I was still able to see so much. It was then that I started focusing on what I could see instead of what I couldn't see. On what I could do instead of what I couldn't do. I started painting using the techniques that John Bramblitt did, built up my confidence and grew from there.

Since I could not see well enough to just paint, I had to think a lot about what I wanted to 'say' in my paintings. What was it that I wanted you to see or feel? I went back to my commercial art days and thought about how I could get across what I wanted to about my painting. I thought about mood, emotion and how best to convey it. This is much more important to me than just making a painting that looks like the reference. If the mood is happy, what colors will make the viewer feel that. If the mood is quiet and peaceful, how can I get that across?

I paint in a somewhat impressionist style, giving you the impression of leaves in the background instead of just painting them. I think this actually makes a stronger statement than just regurgitating what is there already. I can make something more or less important by the amount of detail I put into it. If I were just to paint what I saw, I would lose this opportunity. I also change shapes of things like flower petals to make them more flowing. It is a softer curvier version of reality and I find that it often changes the tone of the painting for the better.

Lastly there is color. I don't stick to the colors that I see in the reference. I will often play around with the image in a photo editor program to get an idea of how I can change them, or bring out more intensely what is already there. A blueish tinge to the fur of a black bear, in my painting, will show much more intensely than in reality. I don't think much of reality anyway. If I wanted it to look the same as the photo, I'd hang up the photo.

Sometimes the colors are changed drastically. I use these colors for emotion, but also for depth. Warms and cools, lights and darks. How you play these against each other changes the painting to say different things. If I paint a portrait, you can pretty much count on the fact that there will be no skin tone color in it. I will use color simply for depth and emotion, pulling forward highlights with warm or light colors and pushing back shadows with cool or dark colors.

People will often ask what type of flower is it that I painted, or what species of bird. I don't pay attention to that information in my references. It really wouldn't matter in the end. Since I change so much, it will not be the exact representation of that species anyway. My flowers will look like flowers, and my birds will look like birds, but that's about it. If I were doing illustrations for a gardening book, this would matter. My stories are about moments. How do you feel in this moment? So the species is not important to this story.

Many people like my style, some don't. I don't worry about it, art is art. What speaks to one person may not speak to another. I even had someone tell me once that a painting that I had done of a young man playing the trombone looked to him, like someone throwing up. Another told me that he could not find the face of a boy in a different painting. I laugh and let it go. There are so many more that have told me how much my paintings have moved them. Some have chosen to live with my paintings, others have just been moved in the moment. That painting of the boy is now hanging in someone's home. They see it and they are moved by it. I am honored to be able to speak to these people's soul.

Just as I thought we were about to make some positive changes to life and things would get easier, I found out that the tumor was growing again and that I would need to go through radiation treatment. For six weeks I went every weekday down to the hospital first thing in the morning. I had five different people that would drive me, each on their day to the hospital since I had stopped driving anywhere but in town. Half way there, I would take some medication to help me to get through it since I am claustrophobic and the procedure required a fitted plastic mask over my face to be secured down to the table. This actually horrified me more than needing the treatment itself. It only took about ten minutes, but they were a very long ten minutes.

The first day I wasn't sure if they were going to be able to get me to go through with it. The mask, made of plastic mesh, had been made to fit my face specifically and covered my entire face. They would fasten it to the table so that I would be unable to move, then, leave the room. I started to panic. They brought Chris in to try and calm me down. The Dr. had told me that they would cut eye holes in the mask. The technicians said not on day one. I was freaking out so badly that they went to get the doctor. He told them to go ahead and cut the holes. I made them make them bigger twice. Finally, they were big enough that I could not see the edges around my eyes and I let them continue. That's when they decided to medicate me. One time, though, I made the mistake of looking up toward the ceiling during the procedure. I was on my back and above me was something reflective. I think it was a piece of glass. I saw my reflection. What a horrifying sight. Seeing the mask on my face spooked me pretty bad. I never looked up again.

After the treatment, I would be dropped off at the gallery. The radiologist had told me that I could still drive and work. I really don't know what planet that doctor lives on, but he certainly has never had radiation treatment. Driving would have been OK, I guess, if I could see, but working, not so much. I was lucky that I ran my own business. I opened the shop and slept on the couch in the back studio until any customers came in. Chris would come after he got done work and we would close up and go home. That was pretty much my day. Weekends were a little better, since I did not get treatment on the weekends. Monday morning always had me feeling pretty good, but then it would start all over again.

I was obviously not creating much during this time. It was all I could do to get through it. I did take to making small stuffed monsters that I called Pet Peeves. They were supposed to represent all those little, but awful things in your life that make you nuts. They were little. They could be thrown, beat up or just set on your desk to remind you that you are bigger than your problems. They went over well at the gallery and I had some way of expressing my grief positively and creatively.

Since they were radiating the area around my throat, my sense of taste got messed up. I simply couldn't taste some things at all. That was not the worst, though. Most things that I did taste, to me, tasted like a stick of air freshener. No, I never ate a stick of air freshener, but you can use your imagination.

Before my taste went south, people were helping us out with dinners. My daughter and her husband were living with us at the time and my son-in-law loves to cook. He actually made my last meal. We didn't know at the time that it would be the last time that I would taste properly, but it was. He made chicken marsala. We came home at dinnertime to find the table set by candlelight. Two glasses of wine at our spots and he served what would be my last meal. It was sweet. I was so glad that I had not wasted that last night of tasting right on reheated chicken fingers.

After that things are a bit of a blur. If people were still helping us with dinners, I don't remember. I would not have been able to eat them. Chris still needed to eat, so maybe they did. I apologize to anyone who helped out in this way that I don't recall. I'm not even real sure how my measly and pitiful meals were being prepared.

I could eat chicken, since it didn't have any taste. Peas and carrots tasted like peas and carrots and I could tolerate a small amount of pasta. Since I also had no saliva, everything needed to be smothered in some kind of gravy, usually cream of mushroom soup since mushrooms also had no taste. This may not sound like such a bad meal, but remember, that was it, every day.

During this time, my 2-year-old grandson wanted to share one of his strawberries with me. He loved strawberries more than any other food. He thought it would make me feel better. I took it from him, put it in my mouth and immediately spit it out. I hadn't expected the awful taste. He felt so bad. He thought it would make me feel better, not worse. It was so hard to explain to him what was going on with me.

Hunger began to mean nothing to me, I just ignored it. I got through by drinking Ensure, half frozen and through a straw so it would go past my taste buds. I drank half a bottle at lunch and the other half in the evening, only because I was supposed to. You would be surprised how easy it is under certain circumstances, for your brain to stop identifying hunger as something to act on. It was sort of like a dull headache. Something that is annoying, but you just keep on through your day basically ignoring it. I was too tired to care anyway. Each night, I slept a good ten hours and then got up and did it all over again.

I have always been an insomniac. I have spent many nights over the years sitting up all night, getting to sleep 3, 4 or even 5 o'clock in the morning. I have tried everything I could to help me to sleep. Unfortunately for me, things that are supposed to help you sleep actually keep me up. I guess in a way, this is good or I might have become dependent on them. During this time, though, I had no such problems. Chris couldn't believe it. The second my head hit the pillow, I was out and there I stayed until morning. I kept a sippy cup of water on my nightstand since I was so dry that I would occasionally wake up with my tongue stuck to the roof of my mouth. This was the only time in my life when I actually slept every night.

Finally, the six weeks were over. It took some time, and some work, but I began to get some of my strength back and started planning the future one more time. The growth of the tumor had been stopped for now. Unfortunately, the taste thing did not go away so fast. I went through several stages with things tasting differently. Since I never really knew what something would taste like, I would often eat standing over the trash can in case I needed to spit it out.

I had one season where everything tasted salty. All I ate during this time was french fries and soft pretzels. These were foods that should be salty. I made sure that there was no added salt on since I didn't need any real salt and to add more would have been extreme overkill. It took almost a year for things to taste right. Even when things tasted 'right' that did not mean that I would feel the same about them as I had before. Like my grandson, I had always loved strawberries. As a kid I would choose strawberry over chocolate, but now, though they taste like strawberries, I can take or leave them. My taste was forever changed. And no, I did not lose a bunch of weight during this time. I came out of this year in the same place I went into due to the Ensure.

My strength also, never got back to where it had been before. I know that I am getting older, and being blind has me less active, but it was night and day. I was probably in the best physical condition of my life before radiation, and ever since I have felt like an old woman. It is 7 years since radiation and I am still working on getting to a better place with my physical condition.

Chapter Five

Adapting to a New World

Out for a Walk – Pittsburgh Aviary Series

The day I had my 6-week follow up appointment with the radiologist, I got a phone call to set up my first appointment with the low-vision optometrist. This is a doctor who helps you with devices to make your life easier, to help you do what you need to do. I was hoping that I would get a pair of sunglasses that would block the glare better to help me drive. The light sensitivity was getting pretty bad, and on sunny days it was getting increasingly more difficult to see things like the color of the traffic lights. I was good in the rain or at twilight, but the bright sun or the headlights of other cars at night made driving pretty frustrating. Regular sunglasses just made everything dark. This did not help at all. I would often get excited to see that we were having a rainy day and use that day to get some errands done. Instead of a magic pair of sunglasses, I was told that I was now legally blind and could not drive at all.

Now it was time to start over once again. I was only driving to and from the gallery and locally in our 25MPH town to run errands like the bank or post office. Our daughter lived close and, having no car, I would drive to her and she would then drive to the grocery store or any other place either of us needed to go once a week. All this had to be rethought.

I found a wonderful woman who lived nearby who agreed to drive me to work each day. She had actually been one of the ones driving me to radiation. Chris would then stop by and take me home on his way home from work. We pretty much just left my car with our daughter. She could then take me anywhere else that I needed to go and use it herself. Sounds great, but having to adjust to this kind of life is not easy. You can never just decide that you need to do something and then go do it. Everything needs to be planned out ahead of time and scheduled with everyone's time in mind.

On the bright side, this is when I got a lot of the devices that help me live a more normal life. To help in my painting, I got an Acrobat. This device uses a pivoting camera on a swing arm and displays the image onto a monitor. There are controls to magnify the image. I used this to help me to see my work. Usually, I take an area about 3" x 5" and magnify it to fil the 24" screen. I then move around the canvas painting each 3 x 5 space until I have covered the whole thing. This requires a lot of back and forth, but the clarity of detail it gives me is night and day to working without it.

My wonderful husband built me an easel that this device attaches to. This made it possible for me to do many things that I could not do before. There are limitations to working like this. I can only work so big since my canvas needs to fit under the camera. Also, I am working on one tiny spot at a time. I can't just easily move from one space to another. It is worth it though. With it I was able to change the way I painted since I could see my work so much better. It opened up so many possibilities and I could tell my painting's story in new ways.

The texture lines that I was using were now optional. Previously, I would outline all the shapes in my painting with dimensional paint so that I would not lose them while painting. This is one technique that I learned from John Bramblitt's story. Now, I will still use the dimensional lines, but only when I want to instead of because I have to. They can add something to the painting. I would never have done it without vision loss. Working around my disability gave me an advantage. It taught me something that I wouldn't have known without it. Also, I previously would have filled in those areas with solid color. Now I was free to blend my colors. My work changed completely and I love what I am now doing.

I also have a device called an Iris Vision. It is a virtual reality type device. It fits on your face like goggles and you see things through the camera on a phone. This allows me to work on the whole painting at one time unlike the Acrobat, since I only have to move my head to change what I am seeing. Unfortunately, the camera quality is not great so details are tough. I also have a pair of magnifier glasses that have some ridiculous power. I need to be really close to the painting to use them, but since they allow me to see what is actually there instead of a camera image, can prove useful at times. I use whichever device suits my purposes. Sometimes more than one device will be used on a single painting.

I have a giant letter keyboard and special software that lets me magnify my computer screen as well as other helpful things like changing the size and color of my cursor. It will also read to me so I do not have to struggle with large bodies of text. It allows me to zoom in on whatever I am doing. You have probably done this while on the internet. I can make things much bigger than will show on my screen. This means that I actually have to pan to see the whole desk top. It drives anyone else who tries to use my computer nuts, but this is what works for me. It is my normal.

I have different magnifiers that help with different tasks. Some of these are high tech, some not. I found that a small 5x pocket magnifier that came from a coin shop for a few dollars is a big help for a lot of things. I leave each magnifier where I use it. I have always hated looking for things and now, with vision loss, really have no patience for it. If the device that I use for a task is right there at hand, life is easier. This means that I have duplicates of some things. Everyone knows not to move my devices. If it is on the end table, that is where it belongs. This was a bit challenging with the grandkids, but they have all come around to the understanding that you do not move Grammy's stuff.

When I first began to lose my sight, I stopped reading. It was just too difficult and eventually impossible. I'm not sure how many years it had been since I had read a book before I started to find these new ways to cope. I first got a kindle and now use an iPad. I am able to enlarge the font, switch to a black background with white text, use an easier to read font and even let it read to me if needed. The ipad has turned out to be invaluable. I use it the way most people use their phone. Internet browsing, face time calls, and e-mail are all done on here.

When reading to the grandkids, they know to bring me certain books and leave the others for Grampa. Some books have much larger print and there are some I have pretty much memorized from reading them to my own kids. I did have a tendency to avoid reading anything to them at first, since I would often struggle with some words. When my grandson started reading, though, I realized that this was a bad example. If he saw me struggle, instead of making him think less of me, he would be encouraged to struggle through also. I think it is important to realize what my actions are telling my grandkids. I don't want them to give up when things are difficult. I want them to overcome their obstacles, so I want them to see me overcoming mine.

I have little bump dots on many things. They go on like stickers and are dimensional so I can feel it and know where high is on the stove or which button is the light on my microwave. I even have two small ones on my phone to tell me where the home button is. This baffled the guy at the Verizon store when I went in for some tech help, but it is what works for me. Sometimes a brightly colored sticker will help, too. When something is hard to see, a spot of color can make it easier to find.

My surroundings needed to adapt to my situation so I could live life more naturally. Of course, new things are always the worst. After a while, you memorize things. You can probably operate your dishwasher or microwave without really paying attention. We all do this. But when you get a new device, you can look at the buttons and see what they do. I can't. I am not good at memorization. New things are tough. These bump dots and stickers can help.

Chris once printed out an enlarged photo of our new toaster oven's controls and laminated it so I could refer to it while I got used to it. (I'm still not used to it.) Every part of daily life needs to be thought out. We even put our living room couch on movable casters so it can sit smack in front of our 50" TV on normal days and spun around to face the rest of the room when we have company. It makes for a very odd furniture layout, but again, it is what works for me.

My granddaughter was born with the interior decorating gene. She is always complimenting or commenting on things around the house. Once when she was about 4, I was sitting on the couch with her while she watched TV. She turned to me and asked if I liked my couch. I said that, yes, it was OK, it was the best we could find at the time we bought it and asked her why she asked. She said, "Because if you move the TV over there and turn the couch, you could see the TV from the whole room." She recognized that we had not chosen this layout for aesthetic purposes. I explained to her that it was because of my inability to see from across the room.

It is not easy getting used to asking for help. Somehow it makes you feel like a child. Every time I need to make a doctor appointment, I have to check the availability of one of my daughters to take me there. I tend to put things off because of this. When shopping I often need someone else to tell me the price or size of something. I carry a magnifier with me, but this can be a hassle. Trying to sort through a rack of clothes juggling a magnifier to see the price and size is a pain. When I have some computer problem even with magnification, it often is just too hard to resolve on my own. I am blessed by a family who is always willing to help, but it is not always easy to need that help.

My son now has Stargardt's as well. He now needs this same kind of help. I know it is not easy for him, since it is not easy for me. Yes, this thing has sure gotten a hold on our family. In order to get this thing, both your parents have to be carrying it. If they are each carrying one bad copy of the gene, each child has a 25% chance of getting it. My parents have 2 kids, we both have it. What then are the chances of one of my kids getting it? Well, Chris would have to be carrying it, too. Even with the early scare that we had with our youngest, we thought this such an outside chance that we assumed it would not be. Turns out, he is. Now, our kids have a mom with two bad copies and a dad with one, giving them a 50/50 chance. So far only one of our kids has it. It doesn't stop there. Chris having the bad gene means that it is in his family, too. He has two brothers and three sisters. One of our nieces has a form of it, so his brother and sister-in-law are both carrying it. Also, his other brother passed down the gene to his son, who married someone carrying it and they have a daughter with it as well. I don't know what the odds are of all that lining up, but we have a lot of sight loss in our family. This does make our family very sensitive to all of our needs.

One place that I do not feel any lacking, oddly enough, is in my painting. This should, I guess, be the worst thing to deal with being legally blind. I paint so much better than I ever did before sight loss that it really doesn't bother me much. That does not mean that it does not bother me. I have been known to throw the occasional fit. Most of the time, though, I just treat it as normal. This is my normal.

Because of my limitations, I cannot make something perfect right out of the gate. This means that I have the freedom to just paint, no worries, no fear. I paint a base layer first. This layer gets the basic painting worked out. Since I will be going back over it, I don't worry about it. I am making decisions about form, color and layout. If I obsess over it at this point and change my mind, I will have wasted my time. Since I am not worried, I just paint. I let things happen. Then, I sit back and decide which things worked out and what I want to keep or change. I usually do this layer with no magnification. Since I know that there is no way that I can make this layer look good, I am totally free to work from my gut, letting things happen. Sometimes you get freebies or happy accidents. These are terms that I use to describe something that happens that you didn't plan. Maybe a bit of pink got into a cloud. Maybe a color got into your water that you didn't intend, making it look like a reflection. If you are too exacting, you can miss out on these.

After this layer is done, I use one or more of my devices to make changes and put in detail. Since I can only see a small area at a time with the device that I use most often, it is very helpful to have the painting base coated in already. I know that the wing of the bird belongs where I am painting it. To try and paint from the get go with the Acrobat would be tough since my placement could be off. No one wants to spend hours painting perfect detail to find out it was in the wrong spot.

I often tell my students that they have the disability of seeing too well. Yes, my students. I still teach painting. My peripheral vision is still normal so I use the portion of my eye below center to see. It makes it difficult to read or recognize people, but I still see enough to help my students. I am often trying to get them to let go, use their gut and leave their brain out of it. Your brain will often lead you astray. I can't tell you how many times I have had to convince students to make the noses bigger in portraits. They are too worried about making a big, ugly nose. The result, though, is a tiny alien looking one. Sometimes they will be stuck trying to figure out what some tiny object in the background of a reference photo is. They will insist on figuring it out. They ask me what I think it is. My answer is always the same. If you can't tell what it is in the reference, why do you want to paint it? It is obviously not important to the story you are telling. This is where I have an advantage. If I can't see something, it is obviously not important to the story. They are stuck in their head, worried and afraid of messing up. The only thing that you can be sure of if you are afraid of messing something up, is that you will. Look at the reference, feel the story you want to tell and let the paint do the work. There will be plenty of time to get your brain involved when you move on to details.

Chapter Six

Opportunities

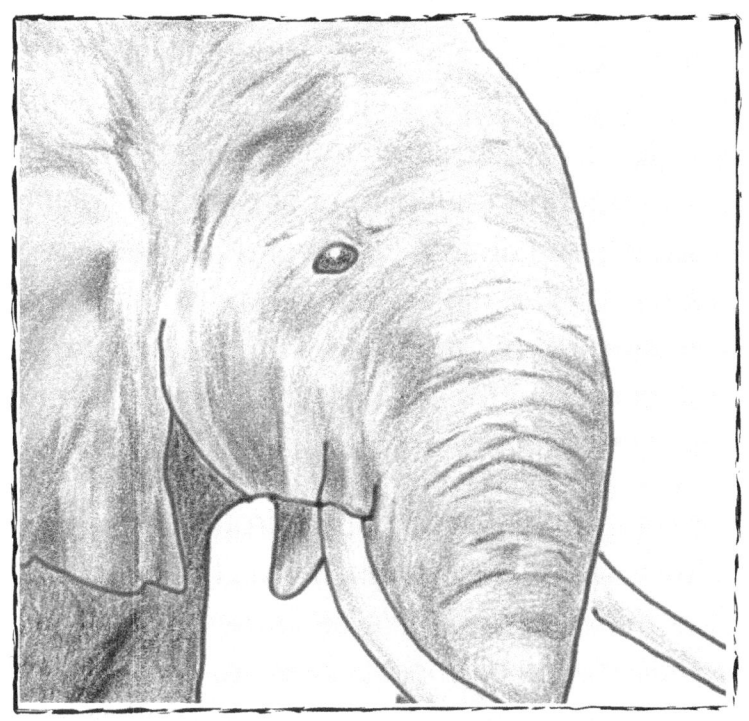

Ellie – See What I See

While our gallery was open, I showed my art there regularly along with that of other artists. We occasionally ran exhibits featuring one artist. During that time and since, I have also exhibited in several art shows at our gallery and other locations. My first was called Faces of South Africa. We held it in our own gallery. This one happened before I got the visual aid assistance, so it was early on in my artistic development post vision loss.

I was using the techniques that I picked up from John Bramblitt at this time. I would draw my subject in a posterized fashion, outlining each shape. I then added a dimensional paint to these lines. When dry, I could see these lines much better than just pencil. They would create shadows making them much bolder. I could even feel them if I needed to. It also kept me from 'losing' my lines. Often while painting, if I covered a line up with paint, I was lost. The dimension stayed so I always knew where my lines were. Of course, you can't change your mind on shape once these lines are there, but they were crucial to my painting at the time.

For reference, I used photos from people who had gone on mission trips to South Africa. I painted emotion. I tried to convey these people as I saw them, happy, contemplative, wise or impressionable. It was interesting how, since I was using such unorthodox colors, only emotion came through. Suddenly race was taken out of the equation. These people were just people, same as all of us, no matter what color we are. They were living in a disadvantaged place and if we lived there, this would be us. They had all the range of emotion that we did. They loved their kids, enjoyed singing and some of them were even shy. It brought them into people's hearts more easily, since everyone was able to insert themselves into each subject, imagining themselves as those people. As unintended as this was in the beginning, I found it to be a very meaningful part of it in the end. I do not believe in separating people by physical attributes. We are all made in the image of God and come from the same two parents. No one should hold themselves over another because of skin color. This to me is as silly as doing so over hair or eye color. This show was a benefit for Casa Ministries. I was happy that the people in the paintings that I created were benefitting from them. The show was well received and I was thrilled to have a story written in the newspaper that was placed on the cover of the entertainment section.

My favorite painting out of this series was one I called Wise Woman. I found a photo of three women on a front porch. This one woman, wearing a big hat and beaded necklace, was kind of hanging back. She was letting the other two have the spotlight. Something about her caught my attention. I wanted to sit down and hear what she had to say. I am sure she had much to tell someone who would listen. I zoomed in on her face and painted her.

This painting was also shown in an exhibit featuring artists with disabilities during The Pittsburgh Arts Festival. I was kind of sad when it sold, but I am happy someone else gets to live with it every day. That is, after all, why I paint. I am thrilled that people actually want to live with something that I created. It is a little bit like hearing that woman's story. They are living with a little bit of my story. When I create my paintings, I do so as if I am painting it for someone else. Maybe a friend or someone who has asked me to paint something for them. I paint it with them in mind. My paintings are made for friends that I do not know yet.

There were other opportunities to share both my art and my vision loss story. I did a show called Vision and Revision with another blind artist at a neighboring Art Gallery and another called See What I See with a different blind artist at the Children's Museum in Pittsburgh. Both of these shows focused on overcoming blindness as an artist and both gave me an opportunity to share with others about vision loss and overcoming it.

For these two shows I was using my magnification devices. This meant that I could paint much differently than before, so my work had changed drastically. Bold colors were still a strong part of my work, but I was now blending colors and the dimensional lines were only occasionally present. I was also able to share more specifically, how to overcome vision loss because of these devices.

The Children's Museum was such a wonderful opportunity. In addition to the art exhibit opening, we went down during regular hours and painted using our magnifying devices. We spent the day painting. People would come and watch. We would chat with them about what we were doing and answer questions. It was a really nice day. The directors at the museum were so helpful and welcoming, they made it a great experience for everyone. It was a great chance to share with others our overcoming story.

One of the pieces that I showed in this exhibit sold to a blind couple. The husband had some vision, but the wife had none. He appreciated my bold use of color, which I'm sure made it easier for him to see. It was an elephant. I used a technique where you sculpt on the canvas before painting. This brings out highlights and shadows making the painting even bolder. The wife, then, was able to feel the painting and understand, at least in a small way, what it was about. On this particular piece, my artistic take on the texture of elephant skin would have been mostly what she would have been able to feel.

I have been working on a technique to make art for the blind. I hope to develop it more and do a show with art made specifically for the blind sometime soon. I would not want to be kept from being an artist due to my blindness and I don't like to think of others being excluded from the art world because of it either. Art can be shared and experienced on many levels. No one should be kept from it. I have seen what is called braille art. This is simply the words blue water in braille embedded in the art. I do not understand how this is sharing anything artistic. Descriptive text can 'paint' a picture, but I don't think this is exactly doing the job. I want a blind person to experience a sunset. Maybe not literally, but in some way to understand the shifts in tones and values. I want to speak to them artistically, not literally.

On a previous visit to this same museum for an artist demo day, I took glasses that we made showing what it is like to go through life with my vision loss. A friend got me some sample glasses from an optometrist that had been discontinued. Chris painted a smear in the center with an iridescent paint that mimicked as best we could what it is like for me to see.

I had the kids at the museum paint while wearing the glasses, explain that I had to do everything with this blur in my way. After they were done, I talked with them about it. I asked them if it was hard. They said "yes." I told them, "But you did it, right?" They said "yes." Then I said that just because something is hard doesn't mean you can't do it. My hope is that when these kids (or their parents who were standing by,) come across some difficulty in life, would remember the glasses and how hard it is for me to paint. Then maybe, they will choose to overcome their difficulty instead of giving up.

These glasses have turned out to be a great way for me to help others understand what it is like for me to go through life. My grandson was always asking me what it was like for me to see. He wanted to better understand why I couldn't see and what it was that I did see. Once in the grocery store, he took a banana and put it on the bridge of his nose between his eyes and asked; "Is this what it's like?" He wasn't far off. He was only about 3 when we made these glasses. I put them on him and told him that this was what it was like for me. He looked one way, then the other. He nodded his head and handed them back. They explained something to a very young kid that words could not. I also keep a pair of these in my studio. When I get a new student or other visitor who is interested in what I am dealing with, I get them out. Many people find it a great insight into understanding my vision loss. It gives them a better understanding of what I can and can't do.

I have had many other opportunities to share with others about my sight loss and my painting. I have been invited to speak at colleges and events, been interviewed on the local TV news and radio. The newspaper has done several other articles on shows that I have done including the children's museum. All of these opportunities have given me the chance to share with others what it is like for me and how I thrive in spite of it. I don't settle for getting by, I want to live complete.

My story of overcoming blindness has the power to speak to many different issues. I don't restrict it to blindness and art. Anything difficult can be overcome. My point is always to keep trying. Find a way over around or through your problem. Don't just lay down and give up, when you can stand and fight. You may lose a battle or two, but keep going until you win the war.

I have also had many opportunities to talk one on one with people. The day I did the painting demo with my special glasses, I was honored to have a family come specifically to see me. A couple brought their grandkids to watch and talk to me since their dad had just lost his sight. He had tunnel vision so his vision loss was actually the opposite of mine, but talking with me helped the kids understand better what their dad was going through.

Many people don't like to talk about their difficulties. It either makes them uncomfortable or they just don't know how to explain it. I have never been at a loss for words, so this is not a problem for me. I love getting the chance to share with others my story. Talking about my difficulties is actually healing to me. I have called it out, named it. Its power over me is less. I cannot get stuck in my head, afraid. I also hope others can see something in my life that will encourage them in theirs. It pains me to think of people paralyzed by difficulties. They have lost so much already. I don't want them to give up even more.

Even the teaching that I do is a way to be encouraging to others. I not only teach art, but as all teachers do, I also am teaching life. I can encourage them to try something new, something hard. I can help them to overcome their obstacles. I have been known to ban the word hard from my students' vocabulary. I don't want to hear about how hard something is. If it is worthwhile, we will try it. I will help them and we will give it the best shot we can. If it works out, they will have won a great battle. If it does not, we will try another way until it does. I hope that they will carry this lesson on into the rest of their lives. I hope that they will learn not to shrink back when things get hard, but to keep going and see it through. There are victories ahead, if they will only move forward to find them.

After six years, we decided to close the gallery. It was not making a terrific amount of money and I was having trouble running the place and being an artist too. Since I could not drive, I couldn't get around to promote the place, so it was hard to draw more attention to it. Blindness was adding to the difficulties in being a business owner, but mostly the amount of time and effort it took to manage the place was keeping me from doing what I really wanted to do, paint. We weren't making enough money to hire a manager, so we made the decision to close up. I continued teaching at home. All of my students stayed with me through the transition. Some have since moved on and some new ones have come my way.

I am happy with working at home. We have moved and I have a nice little studio where I paint and teach. Since I do not have my own gallery, I have less opportunities to show my art. I would show my art at other locations, but with the gallery, there were always paintings of mine on display. I still get out and show my art, but it is much less frequent. I just focus on the next thing. If there is no next thing, then I look for that new next thing. Running a small business at home is much less stressful than trying to keep a shop open. The peace I have now makes it easier to be inspired.

Chapter Seven

Living Blind

Take Flight – Pittsburgh Aviary Series

Over the years, the cheerio in my vision had filled in. There was now no center point where I could see properly. This was actually a good thing, though. Without that center, I was forced to use my peripheral vision. When the clear spot was still there, I kept trying to use it, looking at everything in that tiny little space within the circle. Once it became useless, my brain gave up and tried to find another way. I didn't really need to try to do it. It just sort of happened. When something becomes useless, your brain will give up trying to do it. Now I use the area just below center. Think of it this way, if you look straight ahead, you can still see what is below what you are looking at. You can see it, it is clear, but could you read something in that space? Could you see details about it? The more time went by, the more natural it became and that is how I see now.

Being used to it does not mean that I can see normally in this space. Our central vision is where we see best 3 dimensions. Our depth perception is off somewhat with everything we see outside of it. This means that the visual information that I am getting is somewhat skewed. I can see, but I don't always know what it is I am seeing. Sometimes I think a 12 is a 21. I have a hard time reading words in the middle of a paragraph, things like that. There is too much confusion with all those other words around what I am trying to read. If I make those things very large, or if they are separated from things around them, I have a better chance of understanding them.

Recently I had another downgrade in my vision. It is hard to explain. It is just a little harder to do things. I got myself a white cane and I now use an iPad for many things that I didn't before. I use it for reference photos both for myself and my students. I can zoom in on the photo, making it easier to understand what I am seeing. I can sketch on it, and use it to magnify things. I especially like that I can take pictures with it. I like to use my own reference photos for my paintings. Before, if there was something that I wanted a picture of, I would just point the camera in the general direction and snap a bunch of pictures. I would not even bring it to my eye since that would be pointless. Afterwards, I would look at them on the computer to see what I had. There were times that I was amazed at the photos that I got, but often they were useless. Now with the iPad, I can see what I am taking a picture of. I have a 13" screen, I use it the same way everyone else uses their phone. I get much better photos now since I can tell right on the spot if I got the shot that I wanted. It can be a little annoying to carry around a giant iPad to take pictures, but it is worth it.

The cane was something I felt that I needed since I had gotten terrified of escalators. I had declared that if there was no elevator, I was not going. This seemed a bit unreasonable to me, and since I had told others that hard did not mean stop, I plowed through and learned how to use the cane to help me get around. I got one that telescopes. When it is collapsed, it is small enough to keep in my purse. Since I do not need it all the time, this was the best way for me to make sure that I had it when I needed it. I don't have to anticipate its necessity before leaving the house. It is always there. It is still not fun going down escalators or some staircases, but I do it. Each time it gets a little easier. At least, it scares me a little less.

The cane is also a great way to let others around me know that I cannot see. People do not get frustrated with me when I hesitate on those scary escalators. I used to have some issues with this. If I was standing there, trying to get myself psyched up to step on and someone came up behind me, they did not understand what my problem was and get very impatient. Now with the cane, people will go out of their way to give me some space.

I take it with me to the polls to vote. I don't need to explain anything about my sight. They see me with my cane and immediately switch gears to make sure I have what I need. I had to laugh the last time I voted. They wanted to know if I needed a chair. I guess being blind makes your legs weaker. I have used it at events like open house at my grandson's school. It is funny. Any time a parent sees you coming with your white cane, they grab their kid and pull him to their side until you have passed. I try not to abuse this power.

The main point that I would like to make here to anyone worried about using some sort of assistive device, is don't let it bother you. People are not waiting to judge you based on your white cane, walker or wheelchair. They are usually going to go out of their way to help you. Even if I don't need or want the help, I am always appreciative of their intentions. If they do happen to be judgmental, assuming that I am somehow less of a person, I shrug that off, too. Their judgements are a reflection of them as a person not me. Their opinion of me does not change who I am.

The emotional rollercoaster of being blind is a difficult one to be on. Since I have adapted my surroundings to my situation, I can go about my business for quite a while and not really think about the fact that I cannot see normally. I have my own normal. I do things every day the way that I do them every day. The only problem with that is that when it does hit me, it hits hard. All of a sudden, something is hard or just not possible. This something is nothing terribly difficult, at least not for a seeing person, but it is facing me now, suddenly impossible. Little things can be such big things for me. Having to ask for help with directions on a food container is frustrating. I can't read the mail unless I put it under a high-powered magnifier. This is annoying enough that I just don't do it. I once bought a shelf and was so annoyed because I had to wait for Chris to get home to put it together, not because I couldn't physically do it, but because I couldn't read the instructions.

Sometimes I will be doing something and realize that I need something from the store. There are many shops within 10 minutes of here, but I can't get there. I can't just decide that I need a birthday card and run out and get one. I also can't go to the bank, grocery shop or run other simple errands. I have to rely on others to do those things and I have to plan ahead. There are many people who upon hearing this say, "I can take you" but that is not the point. Think about what it would be like to need someone for every little thing you do. Everything needs to be planned out. I cannot do these little things to get them done even when I have plenty of time to do them. Chris has to make extra stops on his way home from work to do them or others need to take time out of their day to come and take me to do it. This can drive me nuts.

Shopping isn't just about getting there. It is so hard to browse when you can't see. It takes so much effort to make out what I am looking at. There are so many things vying for my attention and I don't know what they are. If I am looking for something particular, that's not as bad. If I know what the thing that I want looks like it is easier to find it. It is a bit like Where's Waldo. You need to focus on what the thing that you want looks like and ignore the things that don't match up. If what you are looking for is medium sized and round, do not stop to figure out what each item is on the shelf. Ignore everything that is not medium sized and round. So browsing is not really possible, making shopping much more of a chore than a fun day out.

Even going out to dinner causes its own anxieties. Menus are tough. I used to take a digital magnifier with me, but so many menus are glossy and the reflections make even that impossible to use. Now, I make sure to know where we are going before we leave the house. I check the online menu and decide before we leave. When I can't do this, ordering becomes a game. (Not a fun one.) Chris will read options off the menu for me. I just take the first one that he gets to that is acceptable. It is just too much grief for him to have to read the whole thing to me. Not for him, but for me. I will just forget as he goes through it anyway.

The new house that we bought was a downsize. We wanted a one-story house with a smaller yard. Something easier to take care of and live in. We have had to do some remodeling in our new house. The plan was to be done in a year so we could live our life and not be married to the house. This is our fifth house and if you count the gallery, sixth remodel. We never buy a move-in ready. I have torn down walls, put up sheetrock, spackled, painted, removed and applied wallpaper. I have also assisted in just about any project from plumbing to electrical to construction, that you could think of. Unfortunately, since I cannot see, and can no longer do many of these things, this has taken us three years and we are still not done. We would be done if I could see.

There were so many things that I would normally have taken care of myself, but when I tried, I made a bigger mess than we had to start with. I cannot even paint a wall without leaving so many missed spaces that someone else will need to redo it. This is leaving Chris to do most things himself. I can help him, but I cannot do it. It really bothers me that sometimes, the best help I can be is to stay out of it. I have been reduced from someone who would take care of many projects on my own to being a gofer, getting tools for someone else when needed and washing brushes. Things you have a child do when they are learning how to help out.

When our daughter bought a house near us, I offered to help her paint. I used to be a very capable person. Now, since I can't see, I can be such a mess. We had my 5-year-old granddaughter sit in the room with me to watch for missed spaces and drips. It worked, but this is definitely not my preferred method of working.

Certain places are hard to navigate as a blind person. Sometimes there are efforts made to make things easier, sometimes not. One place that I have experienced difficulty is art museums. Not a lot of effort is made for the blind in museums. They are there for people to come and look at what they have collected, therefore the blind do not seem likely to be their visitors. If they make any effort, it is often braille tags. Being blind is not always being in the black. There are many people who are, like me, legally blind. This means that I do not have enough sight to function 'normally' but I still have some sight.

Being an artist, I like to see what other artists do. I have gained a lot over the years visiting museums and studying the brush strokes of other paintings. Beyond the bright white rooms being hard to deal with due to light sensitivity, getting close to the art can be a problem for me. Once I set off an alarm because I got too close to a painting. I will suddenly notice guards hanging around, keeping an eye on me, making sure that I am not up to something. I asked one once what the problem was when I noticed that I was getting a lot of attention. He told me that I had tripped the alarm and that I should stay back three feet. I apologized and explained why I was getting so close. He just repeated to me to stay three feet away. Now, I ask when I go in if there is any problem with my getting close and explain my situation. They are usually sympathetic and helpful. Even if they were not, at least they would have advance warning and not come in guns blazing, thinking I was stealing or vandalizing something.

Recognizing people is very difficult for me. If someone is in an unusual place, nearly impossible. If I see someone at church and they regularly attend, I might be able to figure out who they are, but if I see the same person out in a store, forget it. I have even not recognized my own kids in a place that I did not expect to see them. Using the space below center in my vision means that I can see that someone is there. I can tell if they are smiling. I can see the color of their shirt. That space though is part of my peripheral vision. Things are distorted there. My brain cannot put the information together well enough to identify who this is. Making it even harder is the fact that it is uncomfortable to point

83

my eyes too high. I keep the dead space just above someone's eyes. I can see the important stuff while we talk. Doing this cuts off their forehead and hair. This leaves me with even less information to use when trying to figure out who someone is.

It helps to hear a voice, but even then, sometimes I need the person to identify themselves. Some people will do this automatically and this is great. I am never offended when someone does this. Even when I do recognize them, I appreciate their effort to help. I will often just play along when I don't know who someone is. I will greet them when they say hello, do the normal chit chat, give them a hug and then, after they have gone, ask Chris who it was. I'm not sure why it seems rude to me to have to ask people who they are, but I feel like it is. I think I am afraid that they will think that I don't find them important enough to remember who they are. Sometimes I can even worry that people will think I'm stuck up, passing them by and not saying hello. Most people know that I can't see. Sometimes they forget, but they would surely not think me rude for bringing it up and asking who they were. Most of the time, I will still just pretend.

I use things other than just facial recognition to identify people. I know the build of many people as well as the way they stand or move. More distinct people are easier and those I know better, too. Still, picking out my husband in a turnpike rest stop is kind of a nightmare. I am always worried that I will walk up to the wrong person. I have never actually done that, but am not really sure at any distance, so I usually just wait for him to find me.

I actually walked up to a young woman in the grocery store and just before I asked this blonde woman with a baby in her cart and a light colored, cross-body purse what some package said on it, realized that this was not my daughter. I can't imagine what this girl would have thought if I had. I now have a rule when shopping. Do not wander away from me. I had to yell at my Mom once for this. She was surprised that it was a problem. She said she does it to my brother all the time. I told her it was scary to be suddenly alone and have no way to find the person you are with. She went home and asked him how he felt about it and he told her it was terrifying. Why he never bothered to tell her that, I don't know. Cell phones can sometimes come to the rescue, but there are stores that you cannot get a signal in, leaving this option out.

Grandchildren can also prove useful in this situation. If I am at the store with one of my daughters and we might get separated, I keep the kid. I will walk along the end aisle and their job is to look down each aisle for Mommy. They are all happy to help. I even have them read price tags at times. They feel important and my life is a little easier.

Once I was explaining how I can pick out certain people. Some by their hair, others the way they stand. A friend's daughter asked how I can tell if it is her. I told her I don't. If she is not with her parents, no way. She just looks too 'normal' to me. She also changes the way she looks too often. A distinctive hair style and color can make the difference for me.

Recognizing other things besides people is tricky, too. If someone shows me a picture on their phone, no chance. If they tell me what I am looking at, though, maybe. We even recently put a window sticker on our car since picking it out in a parking lot or parked on the street can be tough.

Anyone get irritated at the directions on a cake mix or microwave food? I don't know why they insist on making directions so incredibly small, but I need to keep a magnifier in the kitchen. I have a digital one and a regular 5x that I often use. If someone is around, I will usually just ask. Sometimes, if it is something that will be used a few times, I write on it with a sharpie. I also used a sharpie to write the names of spices on labels that I put on each container. I have printed out all my recipes on 8 ½ x 11 in 24-point font and keep them in a binder instead of the usual recipe card box that many people have. All my recipes are in my own version of shorthand, requiring less reading and are saved on my computer so that I can print them out larger when I have a shift in my vision. I think I have already done this twice.

There are many other things around the house that have white labels on them with large writing in sharpie. Cans of leftover house paint, organizing drawers, file folders and more. This is a very easy way to make my life easier to live. I can pull out what I want just as easy as you can. Also, this does not hinder anyone else. Some of the things that make my life easier can make things more difficult for others. Large print labels don't hurt anyone.

It is important to keep finding solutions that keep me from getting frustrated all the time. If I had to try to use a recipe card each time I cooked, I would get frustrated and maybe stop cooking. Instead, I have changed my surroundings to fit me. Often this is a much better way to cope than changing me to fit the surroundings. This is not always possible, but in my home, I have that level of control. I can make my world adapt to me, at least some of it.

On top of being legally blind, I am also single sided deaf. This is not nearly as big a deal, but can still have its issues. The hearing in my good ear is perfect. If the conditions are right, you might not even realize that I have a problem. I have no way to know, though, where sound is coming from. When it first happened, I would go into a dead panic when my phone rang. My good ear heard it, but where was it? I never realized how much you need both ears. If a sound is very loud, it is probably on my left. If it is quieter it could be far away on my left or close on my right. I make sure to put my phone in certain spots in each room so it is easier to find. In the living room it goes on the end table. In the kitchen, the corner of the counter top. If I was only deaf, I could find it by looking for it. If I was only blind, I could find it by listening to it. What I do now, if I don't know where it is, is stop and turn my head slowly left and right. I listen for it to get louder which helps me to figure out where it is. I have also just gotten used to the time it takes to find it. If I don't make it in time, I can always check the caller ID. No need to panic. When I call out to others "Where are you?" and they answer "Over here." I then ask them where here is. Other people can follow the sound's direction, but I have no clue.

I have a hearing aid that transmits sound from my right ear to my left. I thought this would be so great. I do wear it at events like art openings, but not much else. Since the transmitter actually rests on the back of my ear, it picks up what is behind me the most. It then transmits that into my good ear. Since the receiver is in my good ear, sounds that are on that side are somewhat muffled by the device. This gives a lot of my hearing priority to what is going on behind me to the right. It does keep me from ignoring someone trying to get my attention on my right side, which is why I will wear it at an event, but that's about it.

With two ears, I used to be able to follow more than one conversation at a time. I could be talking to someone in front of me and turn to interject something into a conversation going on next to me. With all my audio from both left and right coming into one ear, it is hard to sort it out. It sort of makes one confusing noise. The hearing aid can still be helpful at times, but I am very selective wearing it. Most of the time, I just make sure that I am in a good place to be able to hear others. At a restaurant, I will make sure the deaf ear is in the corner. Everyone at the table should be on my left or in front of me. I also tell anyone on my right that I am deaf in that ear so they don't think I am ignoring them.

You may be surprised, but there are good things to being single-sided deaf. I can shut down noise. If I lay in bed on the good ear, I can block out or muffle most sound. I sleep much better when I am on my good ear. Adapting to the problems is much easier than with blindness. I certainly would not want to be deaf in both ears, but what I have does not really bother me so much.

What this all adds up to is that I have changed myself and the world around me as much as I can to be able to live in it. It is worth it. The alternative is to be disconnected, depressed and bored. None of that appeals to me, so changes it is.

Chapter Eight

What About Healing?

Awakening

So here I am, an artist, partially deaf, legally blind, nasty brain tumor, horrible tinnitus and a follower of Christ. What do I do with that? Shouldn't I expect healing? Shouldn't I be praying for it night and day? Is there something wrong with my faith that I have not received this healing? Well, I have prayed, I do pray, as others have and do. The thing is, I do not choose to hang on to worry over it. I do not keep anxiety over it in my heart.

When I first discovered the brain tumor and since with the blindness, people, well meaning people, would give me books on healing. I often felt like an 'intervention' could happen at any minute. Someone would feel the need to let me know that I was doing it wrong. God heals and if I had not received that healing, I needed to do something different. I needed to read some book, recite some scriptures, pray some prayer. All these people meant well, they were not meaning to be critical, but it sure felt that way. I even wondered for a long time myself if there was something I was doing or not doing to block my healing.

I believe in healing. I have experienced it in myself and in my family in big ways. This is not a matter of belief as many would make it out to be. I even believed so much that healing was coming due to all the prayers being lifted up on my behalf, that when they called to tell me to report for radiation treatment the following Wednesday, I was shocked. I didn't expect to have to actually do radiation. The MRI that I had previous to treatment was supposed to show that the tumor was gone. People were praying for this very thing. I had peace in my heart about it. This was not just wishful thinking, I believed this would happen.

Unbelief and wrong standing with God can definitely impede a healing, but I was examining myself and could not find these things. Books I was reading (from those well intentioned friends) were basically telling me that if I was not receiving my healing, it was my fault. I was not believing enough. My faith was not strong enough. It all seemed to hinge on me.

This is a really easy accusation to make. All the proof you need to say someone is not believing is a lack of healing. I wonder what would happen to those people's faith if they were suffering from something. Actually, I bet they are. Maybe they aren't blind, but are they near-sighted? Why don't they just pray for healing? Look, everybody really does have something and eventually we do die, so God does not heal everything and we cannot blame it all on unbelief. I have become extremely suspect of anyone with a 12-step plan to healing.

These same books can be very helpful and encouraging. I think it was just the inundation from all fronts. So many people thought it necessary for me to get some information. That this information would change my life. Maybe it could have, maybe they weren't wrong in giving it to me. All I know is how I felt, and I felt very put upon. I felt like I owed it to these people to be healed and to do so from something they said or recommended. Every time I saw these people, I felt like I was letting them down by still being blind.

There were people who were a wonderful support also. I remember once a woman in church stopping to ask me how I was doing. Of course, this happened all the time, but the obligation was always there to have something good to say. At least I felt like it was. It would bring people down so much to say anything else. They wouldn't know what to say or how to act. I just got used to replying to those questions by saying that I was doing well. I would put the best spin on things that I could. This woman, though, looked at me with doubt on her face and said "Really?" There was such a sense of relief in me when she said that. I didn't need to tell her how horrible everything was, but I had just been given permission to be real. No pretending necessary here. I was grateful for those moments when I was allowed to be real.

I know it is tough for people. Knowing what to say and do in a situation with someone who is suffering from something can be hard. Everyone wants to be encouraging. They are uncomfortable with their own inability to make something different in the situation. All they want to hear is good news. They want to celebrate with you. That would be great, but sometimes there is very little to celebrate about. I try to remember when dealing with others who are suffering, that it is not about me. How I feel doesn't matter. I try to pay attention to them. Maybe an encouraging word is what they need, but maybe not. Maybe an acknowledgement of their pain is really what they need in the moment.

So if this was not a matter of unbelief what was going on? After much thought, discussion, research and prayer, this is what I have come to think about it. God is God, I am not. I trust Him end of story. I do not trust in my faith, my belief. I trust in Him. Missionaries go to unstable, impoverished areas at God's bidding to help His people. Does God wish to put them in harm's way? No. Shouldn't God just heal that land? God has His plans and we know squat. We follow God where He leads because He is God and He knows all things. My mission field for now, is blindness. I go where He sends me to do His work. I have opportunities to speak into people's lives that I would not otherwise have. Did God give be blindness so I would have these opportunities, NO! He is choosing to use it, though. You are reading this now because of it. You, I'm sure, would care not one bit about my story without it. So, I trust Him with my whole life not just my healing.

Have I given up on healing? No, I still expect full healing. It may happen here in this life, but if not, it certainly will in the next. A proper perspective will change your attitude in big ways. I will see, I will hear. I will be able to experience quiet. (I think quiet is the thing I am most looking forward to.) I know that, I believe that. I am open to God using a miraculous healing in this life for His glory. I am also open to His using my situation as He sees fit and giving me that healing in the next life. I will only be blind for a short time more no matter what. If He heals me today, great. If not, I can only live this way for a few more decades and then I have an eternity to live whole after that.

I recently saw an image of bubbles. It reminded me of my bubble poem. The bubbles that I envisioned in my poem wandered aimlessly, floating along horizontally, going nowhere. These bubbles, though, were like bubbles under water, floating upward. I am still in a bubble. I still have no control over my bubble, but there is a destination. My bubble has a goal. It is moving upward, getting closer to God. He is my ultimate destination.

Chapter Nine

What Now?

Crown Prince – Pittsburgh Aviary Series

There is a Chinese story of a farmer who used an old horse to till his fields. One day, the horse escaped into the hills and when the farmer's neighbors sympathized with the old man over his bad luck, the farmer replied, "Bad luck? Good luck? Who knows?" A week later, the horse returned with a herd of horses from the hills and this time the neighbors congratulated the farmer on his good luck. His reply was, "Good luck? Bad luck? Who knows?"

Then, when the farmer's son was attempting to tame one of the wild horses, he fell off its back and broke his leg. Everyone thought this very bad luck. Not the farmer, whose only reaction was, "Bad luck? Good luck? Who knows?"

Some weeks later, the army marched into the village and conscripted every able-bodied youth they found there. When they saw the farmer's son with his broken leg, they let him off. Now was that good luck or bad luck? Who knows?

Everything that seems on the surface to be an evil may be a good in disguise. And everything that seems good on the surface may really be an evil. So we are wise when we leave it to God to decide what is good fortune and what misfortune, and thank him that all things turn out for good with those who love him.

Author Unknown

I remember hearing this story so long ago. It has been stuck at the back of my mind ever since. I think this says a lot about how our attitude can change how we see the events that happen in our lives. I could see myself as unlucky because I am blind. If I stay stuck on that thought, I might just sit around feeling sorry for myself. There are many things that I have in my life now that would not be there without this blindness. Do I think I am lucky because I am blind, no. I don't think about luck, I really don't believe in luck. I believe in, I focus on what is real. I am blind, so there it is. Not lucky, not unlucky, just real. Just like I should not let unhappiness steal my joy, I should not let perceived unluckiness steal it either. I did not have a choice whether to be blind or not, but I have a choice what I will do with it, what I will do with my life because of it and in spite of it.

So where am I now, where am I going? For now, I teach art in my home. I still paint and am currently looking for more places to show my art. I have recently started writing due to the prodding of my husband. I am enjoying it and I hope others are enjoying what I have to say. My days are filled with teaching, painting, writing and taking care of a home.

Next year is an MRI year. I get one every other year. Last time there had been no change. We will see what this coming year brings. My last visit the doctor shared that he had been very nervous about me, but he now thought that I might be past it. Tomorrow will bring what tomorrow will bring. I will stay focused on today.

One of my daughters comes by once a week and if I need to go anywhere, she takes me. I schedule doctors' appointments around her visits. She brings my grandson with her, so I get to see him and we have begun art lessons with him. Groceries are ordered and then picked up by Chris. This helps our son as well.

Since Chris drives him to work, he can order his groceries also, and they pick them up at the same time. It is a wonderful world we live in with what is available to us. I do so much of my shopping on-line, saving me the trouble of getting out and having to hunt through stores to find what I want. None of this is easy, but hey, find me someone who says life is easy.

My other daughter is about to move an hour north since her husband is now pastoring a church up there so we will have to be moving our weekly art lessons with her two kids to some kind of spend the weekend thing pretty soon. It is such fun sharing creatively with all the grandkids. I love watching them each grow their inner vision. They are all creative, though they all show it in different ways. I try to encourage each in ways that they show interest and talent. It may be painting, but sewing, baking and writing are also wonderful ways to share creatively with them.

It is interesting to watch my relationships with each grandchild grow as I influence the growth of their inner vision. The oldest spent a lot of time at the gallery starting at birth. He has a very conceptually abstract mind. He used to sit and watch Chris at the gallery working on sculptures. He was only 2 or 3, but would pull up a stool and point to each thing Chris was doing as if etching it into his memory. 'Take one of those, dip it in there, do that to it and put it there.' Over and over again, he would point to each step, memorizing Grampa's actions. Once while I was babysitting him, he caught sight of a painting. He looked at it, turned to look questioningly at me, back to the painting, and then back to me. I simply said "Yes." And he replied, "Mommy?" The painting was one that I had done of his mother. It was one of my earlier pieces, abstract. Only part of the face was visible. His ability to see a person, let alone a specific person, amazed me. He loves all things art, painting, sculpting or whatever else you've got and often has his own ideas about what he wants to do on art class day.

My granddaughter enjoys her art class time with me too, but I noticed early on that she had different interests than her brother. When painting she would often complain of her hand being tired. I soon learned that this was little girl code for "I'm bored." She is much more interested in baking and sewing. Her hands never get tired while doing these. We still paint sometimes, but I am happy to bake and sew with her.

The youngest has his own little individualism. Being an only child, he is very particular about how things are done. He never just slops paint on a canvas. Every stroke is placed with meticulous precision. The funny thing is, he does amazing abstracts. My daughter, wanting a painting for the powder room, will give him a pallet with the colors that she wants him to use and just let him go. He puts each stroke on the canvas purposefully and comes up with some really nice stuff.

The growth of my inner vision started when I was very young. I know that what goes into them now will affect who they are as adults. I hope I can be a positive influence for them as they grow their inner vision.

I don't know where my future path will lead. I only know today, and sometimes that is unclear. I will go where the path goes. I will overcome obstacles. I will make sure to enjoy the scenery along the way, and maybe I will paint some of it.

Epilogue

The Girl Behind the Flower – Mommy?

This story was written BC (before Co-vid) Although I was editing during it, I thought I would let the story end with no mention of it. It is hard to tell a story with no end and the Co-vid era is not over. When something is over, you have a better perspective of it. While in it, bleak times look bleak. This is why I was going to leave it out. I don't have much good to say about it. But I am real, it is real. It is affecting my artistic life. To ignore it seems wrong, so here it is.

I live in an area that was not hit very hard by Co-vid. That does not mean that no one got it. Do not think I am minimizing it if it affected you, your family and friends. It just did not really affect us. The shut down and scare, however, did.

In the beginning we had a lot of anxiety. No one knew how hard this was going to hit. They were telling us millions were going to die. I would spend my mornings watching the news to see what had happened the day before. I was always waiting for that dreadful day when things turned from bad to horrific. When they started shutting businesses down, we got even more scared. Would Chris lose his job? What would happen to our health insurance if he did? What would all this do to our financial future? Chris never lost his job. His company was allowed to stay open, but with a reduced amount of work coming in, they still had to lay off many people. I, though, lost all my students. I lost two shows that I was going to be in. I also lost all opportunities to find new places to show my art and books as well as recruit new students. My daughter had planned to take me around to find some new places to show just as the virus hit. I planned to actively look for new students come the end of the school year. Both of these opportunities were stopped dead in their tracks. In the beginning, I thought it would only be a set-back, but we are so far into it now with no end in sight that it is obvious this whole year is lost.

I am concerned for our country as a whole. We cannot go on like this forever. People are losing their businesses. What will the post Co-vid world look like? Things are being done with an effort to help us short term, but what will happen long term? No one really knows. Since I do not know what the world will look like in another year, I also do not know what my world will look like either. We have been trying to do what we can. We got take-out from restaurants that were not allowed to have dine-in eating, and went back to them when they re-opened. We went ahead with putting a roof on our house. We were going to wait until next spring, but decided that since we were blessed with Chris still having a job and having the money, we would make sure at least one contractor had at least one job. I wish I could buy more at small businesses. Not being able to drive means I buy a lot from large businesses on-line.

We live 6 hours away from family. We visit three times a year and my parents come here three times a year. We have seen no one for 8 months and have no plans to see them any time soon. Also, the daughter who lives near and comes once a week, now doesn't come at all. She has some health conditions that have her concerned about the effect the virus would have on her.

Our son was laid off for six weeks and is back to work. Chris sees him every day, since he drives him to work, and I see him once a month when we go to the chiropractor. Our other daughter has just moved and we have no normal set with them yet, but we do occasionally see them. I am not used to this level of isolation. I am normally somewhat isolated due to my blindness. Since I can't get out on my own, I get out less. This time however, has been on a whole other level. I feel like I am under house arrest. Days and even weeks, sometimes, go by where I see no one but Chris.

After the first 4 weeks, I had two students who opted for face-time classes. This gave me a little to do. Since we went 'green' those two and one other have come back to in person class. The rest are still staying away. Since two of the ones who have come back are on an every-other- week rotation, this means I have two classes a week. As I said earlier, I work better with more to do. My days and weeks are filled with a whole lot of nothing. I even started watching TV. I do not like watching TV by myself. I'm a talker. If I can't make comments on what I am watching, I don't see the point. With nothing else to do, I just talk back to the TV.

105

I am also a purpose driven person. I create to share. I paint so it can hang in someone's home. I write for others to read. It doesn't seem to make any sense to me to create things just to store them, therefore, I have not been creating much during this time. You would think that since I have so much more time, I would be creating up a storm. Nope. I will sit in front of the computer or at the easel and be completely devoid of the will to create. So, I don't.

I have tried to keep myself distracted. There are many things we never got done with our new house. I am getting to some of those final things. I have bought shelves to better organize our office, which allowed us to turn it into an office/music room, painted the stoops and reorganized every closet we have. I have been on-line shopping for little things like bathroom light fixtures that we are installing on the weekends. As long as I am focused on these things, I can pretend, a little bit, that life is normal. The futility of painting a canvas is not staring back at me. We are checking things off our to-do list and that seems worthwhile.

I have good days and bad. On the good days I will still create. I don't want to totally give in to the despair that is trying to get me. My stubbornness is keeping me going. If you have read my book *Boulder's and Breadcrumbs,* you may remember the section entitled *It's Already Over.* The idea is to focus on the future instead of the now. If you hurt your leg, you can focus on the pain or remember that it will not hurt forever. Knowing something will end will make it easier to endure. It has been hard to think this way since sometimes it seems like life will be like this forever, but it WILL be over. I WILL start over one more time.

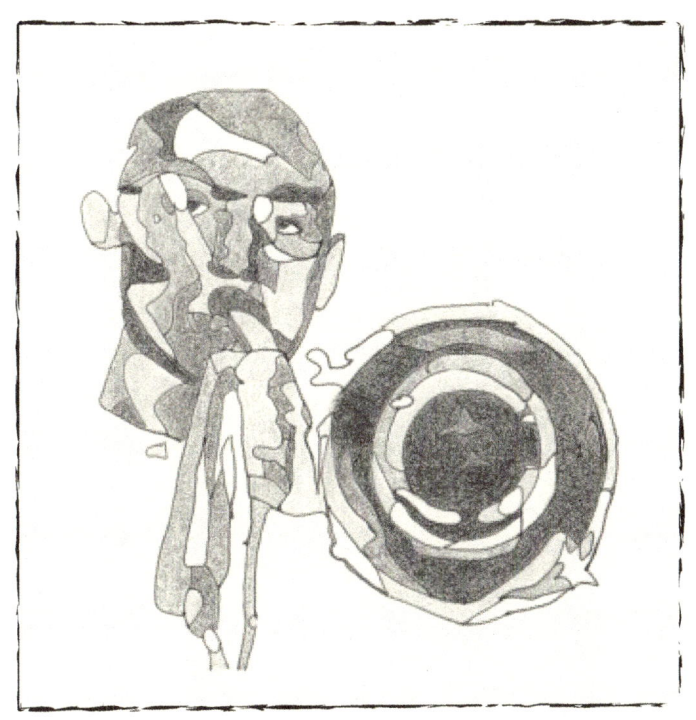

Trombone – aka Man Throwing Up

All sketches were created by Suzanne from her original paintings.

To see Suzanne's work, visit www.suzannegibsonart.info

Made in the USA
Monee, IL
01 November 2020

46530621R00069